Southwell
& Alehouses

Roger Dobson

Roger Dobson

Roger Dobson studied Modern History at Durham University
and went on to a career in education.
He served as a Deputy Headteacher at a
Nottingham comprehensive school for fifteen years.
He married in 1966 and has three children
and four grand children.
He has lived in Southwell since 1978 and since retirement
was elected onto the Town Council.
As Chairman of the Tourism Partnership,
amongst other things he created six local heritage trails.
Recently he was a member of the team that produced
Southwell - the Town and its People Vol.II.
He was a Nottinghamshire magistrate 1994-2007 and is
currently Chairman of Southwell Heritage Trust.

**Nottinghamshire
County Council**

CONTENTS

i

Preface

In the Middle Ages, Southwell Minster was the focus for pilgrimages, and it appears that several inns were built to accommodate the devout visitors, many of whom would have walked long distances. The little town seems to have had a larger number of public houses, in relation to the size of the population, than other places of comparable size. Here is a rich theme for historical research at a local level, and one that Roger Dobson has exploited splendidly. There are a lot of books on local inns and pubs, but few better-researched or more penetrating than this one. Indeed, this book is much more than the story of various historic hostelries; all in all it amounts to an evocation of the diverse social life of Southwell in the past two or three hundred years.

From a wide range of sources, Roger has teased out the diverse roles of hotels, inns and alehouses, and the part they played in the long history of our town. Historically viewed, pubs were not simply places for socialising, drinking and eating out, as many would regard them today: rather were they a focus for early transport developments (especially coaches and carriers), of local commerce (such as auctions and yard sales), of community endeavour (clubs, societies, trade unions, sports teams, musical groups and others) and of popular entertainments. Of course pubs varied in their interests, and the latter encompassed anything from cock-fighting and wrestling matches to cards and 'mummers' theatrical events. At one time or another, pubs were used for such disparate activities as recruiting and billeting soldiers, electioneering, rent collecting (for the Manor of Southwell) and meetings of the Justices. Their history is a rich panorama of the life of a bustling market town.

From all this, it will be clear that the publicans, over many generations, were much more than mere bartenders. Indeed, it is not too much to say that they were leading entrepreneurs, often pursuing a variety of occupations simultaneously. The more successful climbed the rungs of local society to become pillars of the Southwell community. A few, less able or less fortunate, failed to weather the competition and became bankrupt. Assailed by the Temperance movement and the powers of the Justices, publicans' roles contracted in the late Victorian years and early twentieth century.

In this book, however, Roger brings his story up to-date to show how, in our own time, many publicans have recovered something of the spirit of enterprise of their forbears in the hospitality business.

Stanley Chapman
Emeritus Professor, University of Nottingham
Chairman, Southwell and District Local History Society

Acknowledgements

I would like to express my sincere gratitude to the following individuals and organisations who have given me valued assistance during my three year period of research.

I would like firstly to thank Professor Stanley Chapman, Mark Dorrington, Mary West, Pauline Buttery, Tim Warner and especially my wife, Su Dobson for meticulously scrutinising the text, correcting my errors and suggesting ways in which it could be improved. I am also particularly grateful to Terry Pearce for taking many photographs, preparing all the illustrations and designing the front cover. My thanks are also due to Philip Robinson, Mike Struggles and Barbara Masters for their help in locating old photographs. I am indebted in addition to Steve Webb and my daughter Emma Dobson for their technical advice.

I would like to express my gratitude to the following organisations for their courtesy and help with my research and for giving permission to use illustrations and source materials in my book:

Nottinghamshire Archives, Nottingham University Library Manuscripts and Special Collections, Nottingham Central Library (Local Studies Section), Newark and Sherwood Museums Service, Newark Library, the Newark Advertiser, the Bramley Centre Southwell, the Dean and Chapter of Southwell Minster, Southwell Civic Society, Southwell Town Council and Southwell and District Local History Society.

My thanks are also due to the following people for the generous loan of photographs and source materials: Michael Austin, David Birkett, Stuart Blackwood, Grenville Chamberlain, Yvonne and Harry Cooling, Ralph Downing, Larry and Di Dukes, Eric Fower, Robert Hardstaff, Vincent Johnson-Cooper, Rebecca and Brian Jollands, the family of Alfred Loughton, Ann and Raymond Loveridge, John Lukehurst, Pauline Buttery, Anne Reeve, Ruth Robinson, Sue Rodgers, Roland Towers, John Stephenson, Derek Walker, Mary West, Lance Wright and Penny Young.

I am also indebted to the following people for their assistance and advice on specific issues relating to Southwell Inns and Alehouses: Keith Anker, Maria Barnes, Robert Beckett, Molly Broadberry, Dennis Broomfield, Linda Brown, Mrs E Bust, Margaret Church, Steve Church, Rodney Cousins, Gerald Dixon, Geoff Dodsworth, Arthur and Eva Frecknall, Nancy Harrison, Dorothy Hugill, David Hutchinson, Jock Grant, Malcolm Greaves, Andrew Gregory, Herbert Lewin, John and Susan Massey, Christine Measures, Joan Nix, Neil McKechen, Peter O'Malley, Sir John Starkey, Mollie Toy, Alan Whalley and George Wilkinson.

I would finally like to thank local publicans for their assistance and the readiness with which they were prepared to provide information and answer questions.

ISBN: 978-0902751-60-6

Printed and designed by: Nottinghamshire County Council, Design, Publications and Print 2008

1. Why did Southwell have so many inns and alehouses?

From existing evidence, it would appear that over the years there have been at least thirty licensed inns, alehouses, beerhouses and breweries in Southwell. This does not include the numerous wine and spirit merchants which were also licensed premises, or the various alehouses that existed but could not afford a licence. Towards the middle of the nineteenth century, when the local population was only around 3,000, there were up to twenty five public houses. This was before the Temperance Movement really began to affect the growth of the 'drink trade'; an interesting comparison with the ten hostelries which survive today at a time when the number of inhabitants is nearly three times that of 1850. Whatever the period, there has never been any difficulty obtaining liquor in Southwell!

In mediaeval times ale was regarded, with good reason, as a healthier alternative to water. Water supplies were often contaminated and it was quite common for women and even children to drink weak ale. This meant that, apart from the local hostelries, many people who could afford the brewing equipment would have brewed their own ale at home.

It also seems likely that from mediaeval times Southwell's Minster, like other great churches, attracted substantial numbers of pilgrims, most of whom would require food and lodging. According to Malcolm Jones, in *The Secret Middle Ages*, Southwell Minster possessed a supposedly miracle-working cross which would have led to regular Holy Rood pilgrimages. Jones refers to Heywood's *Playe Called the Foure PP* which opens with a long list of shrines commonly visited at that time.

Brewing was a domestic pursuit for centuries.
(Bailey's Household Management *1736)*

At our Lady of Boston at Saint Edmund's burgh...At Redbourn and at the blood of Hales ...
At Master John Shorn at Canterbury The great God of Catwade,
at King Henry At Saint Saviour's, at Our Lady of Southwell...

Other attractions for pilgrims could have been visits to the holy well or to the tombs of saints. RP Shilton in his *History of Southwell (1818)*, refers to an 'ancient Whitsuntide pilgrimage' which both the clergy and laity of Nottingham were expected to complete in accordance with Pope Alexander III's order of 1171.[1] Clearly, regular pilgrimages would have been likely to generate a considerable trade in the town, especially for people requiring accommodation and food, and therefore might explain why there were so many inns in close proximity to the Minster.

A further reason why Southwell has had so many inns and alehouses lies in the popularity of the customary fairs, markets and horse races which were held in the town, particularly on the Burgage. People from neighbouring villages would flock into the town with the Whitsun Horse Races being especially well attended, as is suggested by this newspaper notice.

SOUTHWELL BURGAGE RACES.

THERE will be a PONY RACE on Burgage Green, Southwell, on Whit-Thursday, for a Saddle and Bridle; the best of three Heats.—Ponies not to exceed Twelve Hands.

Also an ASS RACE for a Tea Kettle (a free Prize).

The Ponies to start at Four o'Clock; and the Asses after the first Heat.

For Particulars enquire of John Elsam, White Swan, where the Ponies are to be entered the Day preceding.

Southwell, May 10, 1815.

(NJ May 13 1815)

Large celebrations of major religious and secular events seemed to be very common in the eighteenth, nineteenth and early twentieth centuries. These celebrations would draw people into the town from the neighbouring villages as well as from Southwell itself.
(Southwell Civic Society).

Celebrations of major events were observed far more commonly than today. Royal births, coronations and the king's birthday were usually celebrated with great gusto as were key military victories on land and at sea. These communal celebrations resulted in a big demand for food and drink. A newspaper notice in 1814 about the *'Peace Celebrations'* illustrates this point.

Inns were also the traditional venues for meetings and annual dinners of the vast number of local clubs and societies, ranging from groups of clergy, freemasons and military societies to friendly societies, trade clubs and floral societies. They were also the centre for most of the sporting activity in the town. In the absence of specialised facilities such as a leisure centre or individual clubhouses, publicans were keen to promote sports on their premises. The *Crown* and the *White Swan* were heavily involved in promoting cockfighting, providing the pit, pens for the birds and of course refeshments.[2] The *Crown* was also the centre for prize-fighting and the publicans at the *White Swan* promoted horse racing on the Burgage. It wasn't until later in the nineteenth century that alternative premises to inns began to be developed for meetings and sporting events.

> **FESTIVITIES IN CELEBRATION OF PEACE.**
> The celebration of the glorious events of the present era, has been carried on at Southwell, in this county, on an extensive scale, and in a very spirited manner. A liberal subscription being entered into by the inhabitants, which amounted to near £200. a dinner of roast beef and plum-pudding, with plenty of good ale, was provided on Burgage Green, on Friday last, the 17th instant, of which upwards of one thousand persons partook. The band of the Southwell Regiment of Nottinghamshire Local Militia played during the repast, the effect of which, added to the fineness of the day and the regularity and order with which it was conducted, left an impression on the minds of the spectators never to be effaced!—In the afternoon, an effigy of Buonaparté, mounted on an ass, was conducted round the Green, which, after enduring the execrations of the surrounding crowd, was precipitated into a large bonfire, as a suitable reward for tyranny and usurpation. Various amusements, such as racing, jumping in sacks, dancing, &c. were afterwards exhibited; and in the evening a display of fire-works, consisting of rockets, Roman candles, &c. were let off for the gratification of the company present. A new flag was hoisted upon the Minster, which is to remain as long as a remnant exists.—Not the slightest accident occurred the whole day, and the utmost harmony and good humour prevailed throughout.—On Saturday there was a public dinner at the Assembly Room, which was numerously attended; and on Tuesday evening a ball.

Town Festivities on the defeat of Napoleon Bonaparte in 1814 (NJ June 25 1814). The joy was short lived, however, since Napoleon escaped from Elba and Britain was once more plunged into a war with France, leading to the battle of Waterloo in 1815.

Another contributing factor to the growth of alehouses was the consequences of the 1830 Beer Act. Parliament was concerned about the high level of gin drinking and its effect on the working classes, so they passed a law which encouraged people to drink beer rather than gin. This was achieved by abolishing all duty on beer and establishing the right of any householder to sell beer upon the purchase of a two guinea licence from the Excise Office. Whilst these 'beerhouses' were not allowed to sell wine or spirits, the legislation did lead to a dramatic increase in the number of licensed premises in all areas of the country. In 1830 alone 24,000 licences were taken out.

Beerhouses quickly attracted a number of nicknames. The most common was 'Tom and Jerry' shops, either after two well known London characters or owing to the fact that many beerhouses were made of insubstantial materials. In White's *Trade Directory* of 1832 nine beerhouses are shown in Southwell, representing a dramatic increase in the number of licensed premises. Several of these Southwell beerhouses were located in workshops where the craftsmen could sell the ale as a refreshment for waiting customers.

However, by the middle of the century the Temperance Movement's strong opposition to the drink trade had begun to influence central government's attitude to the growth of public houses and in 1869 the beerhouses, like all public houses, had to apply to the local magistrates for licences. As magistrates were becoming more strict about awarding new licences, it seems that in Southwell, as elsewhere, some beerhouses closed, whilst others raised their status to public houses.

Emergence of Beerhouses in Southwell following the 1830 legislation

Date	King St.	Bar Lane (Queen St.)	Westgate	Westhorpe	Back Lane (Burgage lane)	Maythorne
1832	1	1	3	3	1	-
1835	1	-	3	3	1	-
1844	-	-	1	2	1	-
1853	-	-	-	2	-	-
1864	-	-	2	2	-	1
1872	-	-	1	1	-	1
1881	-	-	1	1	-	1

2. The Hierarchy of Inns and Alehouses in Southwell

Throughout the East Midlands there was a clear hierarchy of inns and alehouses and Southwell was no exception. At the top of the hierarchy were the 'county' inns where the local gentry and fashionable social sets frequently met. The *Saracen's Head* was undoubtedly a county inn. Inventories of two innkeepers from 1622 [3] and 1683 [4] demonstrate that the fixtures and fittings there were unquestionably luxurious and there is evidence that the provision of the accommodation and stabling was improved to meet the rising expectations of customers. In the period after 1820, when it was substantially altered, the *Crown* aspired to move up the social scale and join its rival as a county inn. It probably achieved this objective, as by 1830 it was a successful coaching inn which was holding auctions of superior property, industrial workshops and luxury goods on its premises.

The **Saracen's Head** *was one of the most prestigious 'county' inns in the East Midlands. It attracted many travellers from the upper classes, including royalty and was popular, as a meeting place, with the local gentry and fashionable social sets. (Southwell Civic Society)*

Next in line were the '*secondary*' inns which, in addition to catering for the needs of the local gentry, had close connections with the wholesale and retail trading of their communities and, from the 1770s onwards, showed enterprise in running numerous coaching services. The design and internal layout of these secondary inns would be based on either a 'gatehouse' or a 'courtyard' plan. In the case of the former the main rooms fronted onto the street with a yard to the rear, often accessed from a lane behind. With the courtyard plan, the central yard was enclosed by two or more storeys of public and private rooms. Around 1800 there were arguably four town inns that fitted this category – the *Admiral Rodney,* the *Cross Keys*, the *Castle* and the *Reindeer.* In the early 1860s they were joined by the recently built *Newcastle Arms* whose interior, yard and outbuildings would serve the railway, coaching and omnibus businesses that ran between Southwell and Newark. All these secondary inns provided accommodation for travellers.

Further down the hierarchy came the unpretentious '*carrier*' inns with reasonably sized stabling and much used by local labourers, wagoners and packmen. Carrier inns were important bases for the carriage of goods, with yards available for the storage of goods and rooms for the carriers to meet their customers. For long distance carriers some inns offered accommodation. Whereas coaching declined with the coming of the railways, carrying remained an important service until the end of the nineteenth century. Foremost amongst these carrier inns were the *Black Bull*, the *Wheatsheaf*, the *Portland Arms* and the *White Swan*, all of which were situated on the west side of King Street and all possessing decent sized yards for horse drawn transport. The yards of these inns, especially the *Black Bull* and the *White Swan* were the location for a wide range of trades such as butchers, blacksmiths, wheelwrights and chandlers. Renting outbuildings to these tradesmen would provide innkeepers with valuable additional income.

Next in the social scale would have been *smaller public houses* which were chiefly situated in the hamlets of Easthorpe and Westhorpe. In the long period between 1700 and 1920 these smaller houses acted as centres for the numerous agricultural labourers, framework knitters and skilled and unskilled craftsmen who lived there with their families. Examples of these smaller public houses are the *White Lion (Old Coach House)*, the *Hearty Goodfellow* and the *George and Dragon (Bramley Apple)* in Easthorpe and the *Lord Nelson (Dumbles)* and the *Grapes* in Westhorpe. By the middle of the nineteenth century most 'locals', as these smaller public houses were generally known would have a simple design of a tap room with bar and a smoke room or snug. In the tap room there would have been traditional public house furniture, such as deal tables, wooden forms and wooden settles round the walls. The smoke room would have had slightly better quality furniture and softer seating.

Sketch of a fourteenth century alehouse, ale stake, ale wife and pilgrim. Pilgrims would be regular visitors to the town, especially through the mediaeval period.

Finally, at the bottom of the scale, in the 1700s was the large number of *alehouses* of which little is known. Alehouses took many forms but many would have been simple domestic dwellings thrown open to the labouring poor to drink in the kitchen or parlour, where you could expect to find a fire, stools, basic table and chairs and brewing gear. In many cases the alehouse would have been the haunt of people who could not afford a fire or light in their own rooms. We have no detailed knowledge of local alehouses but it is likely the *Boot and Shoe*, on the Burgage, and the *Bear* in Westgate were alehouses that fitted the description given above.

Following the 1830 Beer Act many of these alehouses became known as *beerhouses* or *beershops*, after the law which encouraged anyone to open a dwelling to sell beer upon the purchase of a two guinea licence. It was a controversial law since many publicans saw the new beerhouses as a competitive threat to their interests. Further opposition focused on the threat to public order that the large number of new drinking places posed. Beerhouses were generally similar to alehouses in size, being often simply a one room property, but they differed in that they were frequently situated in a craftsman's workshop, where ale could be sold to waiting customers. Of the nine beerhouses that were established in the 1830s [5], Mary Fairholm's beerhouse opposite the *Grapes* and Joseph Stanfield's beershop in Back (Burgage) Lane lasted the longest.

In addition to these public houses there were two town *breweries*. The first of these, *Westgate Brewery,* opened in 1876 and continued until 1931. It was later replaced by the Ideal Cinema. In its last years the brewery served more as a distribution centre for Marston's public houses. The second brewery, the *Southwell Brewery Company,* was in the town centre, close to the *Admiral Rodney,* and had a short existence from c.1880-1906.

Making up the thirty premises was a *workman's institute* in Westhorpe, the *Workman's Rest.* Opening in the middle of the nineteenth century it was almost certainly, for most of its existence, a temperance building, but there is evidence to suggest that in its later days the management made an agreement with the *Grapes* to sell its beer.

As well as these thirty premises where beer could be obtained, there was a considerable number of *wine and spirits merchants* in the town which were also licensed premises. These included Kirkby's, Bates', Chadburn's and Rumford's.

Westgate Brewery to the left of the picture, in the early 1900's. Note the brewery sign on the wall. (Southwell Civic Society)

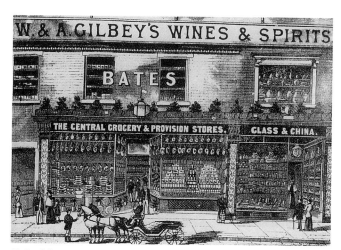

Bates' Grocery and Provision Store, 16-18 King Street; just one of several wine and spirits merchants in town.

3. The Role of the Inns in the Commercial Life of the Town.

There was a dramatic improvement in transport in the late eighteenth century with advances in road making and in vehicles themselves, both contributing to greater mobility amongst all levels of society. More people were travelling for business and pleasure and inns began to provide yards and stabling for the use of carriers and coaching services.

Robert Morvison, carrier to Nottinghamshire and Lincolnshire villages, in 1857.[7]

Both long and short distance carriers operated from the inns, thereby providing rent for stables and warehousing. Carrier and innkeeper worked in close partnership. The *Derby Mercury* of June 1765 records that a carrier called William Holmes conveyed goods and people from and to Southwell. He charged adult passengers two shillings a head and for heavy goods he charged one shilling a hundredweight [6]. After 1790 it was the 'short distance' village carriers that saw an enormous increase in business, linking up with the long distance coach termini. Many, like William Wilson in 1792, commenced business at a Nottingham carrier inn, (the *Crown Inn* on Long Row), and travelled regularly to Southwell. Like many village carriers, William Wilson often transported food parcels and acted as a grocery deliveryman. It is likely that some Southwell innkeepers themselves conducted a subsidiary carrying business to nearby villages, offering a small parcels service and leaving their wives to look after the inn.

Name of carrier	Carrier base	Likely public houses used by carriers	Service
William Revill	Westhorpe	*Lord Nelson*	Nottingham, Newark
John Fryer	Westgate	*Reindeer*	Nottingham, Newark
William Gibson	Westgate	*Shoulder of Mutton*	Nottingham, Newark
William Cooling	King St.	Any of the following- *Black Bull* *Portland Arms* *Wheatsheaf* *White Swan*	Mansfield, Newark
Henry Fearn	King St.		Mansfield, Newark
George Draycott	King St.		Nottingham
Robert Harvey	King St.		Nottingham
Samuel Smedley	King St.		Mansfield, Newark
John Whitlam	King St.		
Joseph Pilgrim	Easthorpe	Any of the following- *Hearty Goodfellow* *George and Dragon* *White Lion*	Nottingham, Newark
John Rickett	Easthorpe		Nottingham
Jeremiah Waterhouse	Easthorpe		Nott'm, Newark, Mansfield

A clear insight into the carriers' journey from Nottingham to Southwell is found in the *Reminiscences of Richard Fisher 1878-1966.*

It would take the carrier three hours or so. He had to call at farms delivering and picking up parcels and getting them to their owners. Often our John was not at home 'til eleven o'clock at night on Saturdays. Those parcels were all delivered on Monday.

The birth of the coaching age in the later 1700s greatly increased commercial activities at Southwell's inns. Changes in coach design, such as the use of steel springs, improved road making techniques, and the spread of Turnpike Trusts all contributed to the growth of commercial traffic in and around the town. The creation in 1759 of the Leadenham to Mansfield Turnpike, linking the town with Newark and the historic Great North Road was particularly important in this respect. Coach companies could also use the road to Nottingham which, although not a turnpike, was generally of good quality. With their residential accommodation, yards and stabling facilities, inns were the natural ports of call for coaches in need of a change of horses and travellers in need of food and lodging.

TOLLS

TO BE DEMANDED AT

Farnsfield Bar,

Upon and from the 6th Day of April, 1814.

(Pursuant to Act of Parliament.)

	S.	D.
For every Coach, Landau or Hearse, drawn by 6 Horses -	2	0
Ditto - - - - - - - 4 Horses -	1	6
Ditto - - - - - - - 2 Horses -	1	0
Ditto - - - - - - - 1 Horse -	0	8
For every Waggon &c. with Narrow Wheels, and drawn by		
- - - - - - - 4 Horses or more	2	3
Ditto - - - - - - 3 Horses -	1	6
Ditto - - - - - - 2 Horses -	0	9
Ditto - - - - - - 1 Horse -	0	6
For every Waggon &c. with Broad Wheels, and drawn by		
- - - - - - - 4 Horses or more	1	6
Ditto - - - - - - 3 Horses -	1	0
Ditto - - - - - - 2 Horses -	0	6
Ditto - - - - - - 1 Horse -	0	4
For every Horse &c. not drawing - - - -	0	1½
For every Drove of Oxen at per Score - - - -	0	10
For every Drove of Calves &c. ditto - - - -	0	5
For every Pair of Millstones - - - -	3	0

Double Toll on Sundays.

☞ Passengers paying the Toll at this Bar, and intending to proceed through KELHAM BAR on the same Day, may procure a TICKET here, which will enable them to pass through such Bar TOLL FREE.

GEO. H. BARROW,

Clerk of the Western Division of the Leadenham and Southwell Turnpike Road. residing at Southwell.

2d April, 1814.

S. AND J. RIDGE, PRINTERS, NEWARK,

Table of Tolls chargeable at Farnsfield Bar on the Leadenham- Newark-Southwell-Mansfield turnpike, 1814. These tolls would have been displayed on a board. (NA DD/111/108/1)

In response to this potential for increased trade, it would seem that the innkeepers displayed a keen entrepreneurial spirit from a very early stage. By the beginning of the nineteenth century innyard paving, stabling and coach house facilities had been greatly expanded at the *Saracen's Head*, the *Crown*, the *Admiral Rodney* and, a little later, at the *Reindeer*. In addition to these larger inns, some of the smaller public houses were clearly determined to get in on the act. From about the middle of the eighteenth century local inns began to offer the facility to hire a post-chaise. In 1769 one local newspaper noted, '*A genteel Post-Chaise, with able horses may be had at George Botham's Black Bull Inn, Southwell to travel to Newark, Nottingham and Mansfield*'. [8]

An insight into what it was like to travel by coach in 1772 is given here in G.Henson's *History of the Framework Knitters (1831)*.

> *Travelling then was much slower than at present; the Nottingham stage coach started at five o'clock on Tuesday morning, the passengers slept at Northampton, and arrived in London at seven o'clock on Thursday evening....A coach that travelled sixty miles a day was termed a 'flying coach'. The fare was about 1s. for five miles, or 25s. from Nottingham to London. The general mode of travelling was by hiring horses at 3d. per mile and for the post-boy conducting 4d. per stage.*

*The **Saracen's Head**, with the new Assembly Rooms next door, and the Crown in the period between 1805 and 1820. Very soon after 1820 the **Crown** was modernised and extended to cope with the increased coaching trade. Note the columns and arcade in the old **Crown** which offered various traders space and shelter.*

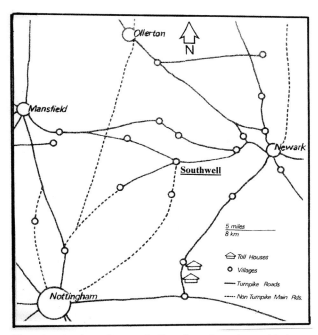

Map showing turnpikes and other decent roads, usable by coaches and carrier waggons in the Southwell district.

By the early 1800s trade directories show that coaches were a regular sight in Southwell. An advertisement for the Minster Grammar School in 1821 boasted that *'Coaches pass daily through Southwell to every part of the Kingdom'*.[9] The centre of the town would therefore have been a lively, bustling place with plenty of staff at the inns and public houses dealing with the needs of the coachmen, their horses and passengers. The table below demonstrates the impact of coach travel on the town inns.

For the coaching trade the arrival of the railway, from the 1840s onwards, signalled the end of an era. Wherever a line was opened, the immediate result was the cessation of local coach services, which could not compete for speed, comfort, cost or capacity. A study of the transport information in the Nottinghamshire Trade Directories shows that this sudden decline in coaching applied to the Southwell-Newark area as well.

By the end of the nineteenth century there had been a further decline in commercial activity in the inns with the continued growth of specialist accommodation in warehouses, exchanges, shops, auction rooms and solicitors' offices. Evidence from local newspapers show that this national trend also applied to Southwell.

Stage Coaches at Southwell Inns 1780-1850		
Stage Coach	**Route**	**Inns providing service**
Accommodation	Birmingham-Newark	*Crown, Saracen's Head, Reindeer*
Hark Forward	Lincoln-Buxton	*Crown*
Magna Carta	Nottingham-Lincoln-Hull	*Saracen's Head*
Champion	Manchester-Lincoln	*Crown, Saracen's Head*
Celerity	Nottingham-Lincoln-Barton	*Crown*
Tally Ho	Manchester-Newark	*Crown, Saracen's Head*
No Wonder	Nottingham-Southwell	*Saracen's Head*
Royal Mail	Mansfield-Newark	*Crown*
Standard	Derby-Newark	*Admiral Rodney*
Queen	Nottingham-Gainsborough	*Saracen's Head*
Imperial	Nottingham-Hull	*Crown*
Negotiator	Nottingham-Newark	*Admiral Rodney*
Diligence	Nottingham-Lincoln	?
New Coach	Derby-Lincoln	?
Pilot	Nottingham-Newark	?
Omnibus	Mansfield-Southwell	*Saracen's Head, Reindeer*

4. The Innkeepers

Some innkeepers – albeit a minority - would have been amongst the wealthiest members of the town, residing at inns higher up the hierarchy. In June 1794, at the outbreak of the war with Revolutionary France, seven Southwell innkeepers were sufficiently well off to donate subscriptions for the purpose of raising a corps of cavalry.[10] Most innkeepers, however, would have found the business far from profitable. Very few inns were owner-occupied as it was much more usual for their owners to be the county and town gentry or wealthy tradesmen. By the late nineteenth century these owners had sold their licensed premises to the big Nottinghamshire breweries.

For most landlords and innkeepers therefore, multiple employment was essential, which often meant that the landlord's family would be involved in the daytime running of the inn. Trade directories and census returns show that some of the landlords' secondary occupations were obviously linked with their primary role as innkeepers, such as working as maltsters and coachmen. On the other hand some of the innkeepers' secondary occupations had little connection with their primary role of innkeeping ; a Fire Insurance document of 1781[11] for instance shows that James Maltby, a local innkeeper, was also a chandler and it was quite common for others to work in trades as blacksmiths, saddlers or bricklayers.

Where the publican pursued another occupation it was his wife who was left to run the pub. This business partnership of man and wife was acknowledged by the authorities in spite of the widespread Victorian view that decent women should not be seen in public houses. There are many instances over the years in local inns and public houses where women publicans established a reputation for being models of efficiency and for keeping order much better than their husbands. Innkeeping was very much a family trade with children and other relatives regularly helping out. Innkeeping sometimes passed down the generations: the Horsley family at the *White Swan* and the Johnson-Coopers at the *George and Dragon* and at the *Hearty Goodfellow*, for instance, can be identified as innkeeping 'dynasties'.

A major grievance for many innkeepers in the eighteenth and early nineteenth centuries was their obligation to assist in the recruitment of soldiers, either by signing up volunteers or through impressment. In 1796, during the French Revolutionary War, fifty-five recruits were required in the Southwell area and fines were to be imposed if they were not forthcoming.[12] An even greater grievance was that innkeepers had a further obligation to quarter soldiers and sailors. Officers would be billeted at the county inns (the *Saracen's Head* and the *Crown*) whilst private soldiers had to make do with the alehouses. This practice was very much a burden on innkeepers as the allowance they were offered was inadequate and they were also expected to provide free beer! The third major complaint for Nottinghamshire innkeepers at this time was the heavy taxation on ale. All three complaints are apparent in this 1772 petition to Parliament.

From the mid nineteenth century innkeepers faced yet another problem. They could no longer assume that magistrates would renew their annual licence. An increase in religious fervour and the growth of the Temperance Movement caused local magistrates to consider restricting victuallers' licences. The licence itself was granted for only one year and was subject to certain conditions such as there should be no adulteration of the beer and no drunkenness on the premises. Houses also had to close during church services on Sundays. This change in the official attitude did eventually lead to the closure of two Southwell public houses soon after the turn of the nineteenth century.

To the Hon. **William Howe**, and **John Plumptre**, Efq; BURGESSES in *Parliament*, for the Town and County of the Town of NOTTINGHAM.

Gentlemen,

WE the Inn-keepers of this Town, (who make a fmall Part of your Conftituents) beg Leave to recommend the inclofed Petition, to be by you prefented in due Form, to the Houfe of Commons ; and we alfo beg the Favor of your Intereft and Support, in promoting a Bill, or a Claufe in fome public Act, for our Relief.

Our Hardfhips, Gentlemen, are really great ; and we wifh not to trouble you with a long Detail of the many Grievances we fuffer in common with our Brethren the Retailers of Ale, &c. but only at this Time point out a few of our Complaints, to furnifh you, (if neceffary) with proper Arguments in our Favor.

The additional Duty laid on Ale, in the Time of Mr. PITT's Adminiftration, is a Burthen that falls entirely on the Publicans ; and we, and others of our Fellow Subjects, much wifh to have that Duty more equally laid, by a General Tax on all Confumers of Malt ; but there is Gentlemen, another real Caufe of Complaint very hard indeed to bear ; and that is, we pay a Duty for all the Beer, the Laws oblige us to give Gratis to the Soldiery. And the high Advance made in the Price of Hay and Straw are fo great, that without Exaggeration, it may truly be faid, the Inn-keepers here, have funk from one Hundred, to forty Pounds a Man fince the quartering of the Horfe upon us in July laft ; fo that befides the general and notorious Hardfhips, which every Publican daily feels, by the quartering of Soldiers, the Innkeepers bear much more than an equal Burthen with their Fellow Subjects. We therefore humbly folicit the Exertion of your well known Abilities, in our Favor, and we doubt not of your hearty Concurrence to remove the Hardfhips complained of in the Body of our Petition ; and hope the Legiflature will lighten them, either by encreafing the Pay of the Horfe, building of Barracks for the Ufe of the Army ; or by fome other Mode, as the Wifdom of Parliament fhall think moft proper, for the real Service of the Community, and of

GENTLEMEN,

NOTTINGHAM APRIL 27th, 1772.

Your diftreffed humble Servants.

A Petition to the House of Commons by Nottingham Innkeepers in 1772. Southwell innkeepers, equally, had grievances on the level of taxation and the obligation to provide for the quartering of soldiers. (NA DD/512/1/2)

Example of an annual licence granted by magistrates to Ale-House keepers in 1782. By the mid nineteenth century magistrates became more questioning when annual licences were sought.
(NA DD/473/1)

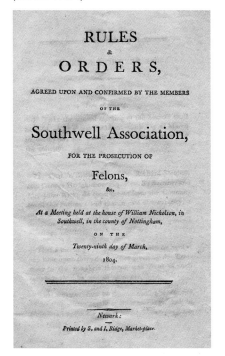

*Inns were centres for the conducting of public administration. The **George and Dragon** served as the headquarters of the 'Southwell Assocation for the Prosecution of Felons'.*
(NA DD/M 71/198)

Despite the hardships of taxation, recruitment and quartering, innkeepers nevertheless remained a powerful and highly influential sector of the community. As well as putting their premises forward as trading centres, innkeepers would also offer services equivalent to our social and leisure clubs. The more fashionable county inns, such as the *Saracen's Head*, the *Crown*, the *Admiral Rodney* and the *Cross Keys*, would have been frequented by the gentry and the professional classes. Their innkeepers were quick to promote dinners, dances, lectures and concerts for this privileged clique whilst local society meetings would also have taken place at these inns. In the early 1800s the Lord Lieutenants, the Clergy Charity, the local Regimental Officers and the Justices of the Peace all met regularly at the *Saracen's Head.* [13]

Town inns and alehouses were centres for sporting entertainment. Arguably the most popular attraction was cockfighting, closely followed by boxing. Consequently innkeepers keenly promoted and publicised big matches, often for a large purse, in front of gentry and working class spectators. Travelling theatrical shows also attracted large crowds to the innyards at the *Saracen's Head*, the *Crown* and the *Admiral Rodney*.

Innkeepers and landlords would be also keen to rent out rooms to working men meeting as a club, usually as a Friendly, Benefit or Charitable Society. Prior to the Welfare State these societies were a means of practical self-help for the working classes against times of unemployment, ill health or old age. At public houses, regular subscriptions would be collected and, when needed, benefits were paid out to members to help settle medical bills and funeral expenses. A public house, as well as offering a relatively cheap and congenial rendezvous, was often the only place with large enough rooms, available for clubs and societies to hold meetings.

Many innkeepers were highly innovative individuals and, in the absence of specialised public buildings such as law courts, post offices, council offices and barracks, promoted their premises as centres for the conducting of public administration. One example of this was the way in which two of the publicans at the *George and Dragon (Bramley Apple)*, William Nicholson and George Revill acted, not just as hosts for meetings of the Southwell Association for the Prosecution of Felons but were leading members as well.[14] Equally, successive innkeepers at the *Saracen's Head* in the middle of the nineteenth century provided a headquarters for the Inland Revenue Office, the Post Office and Southwell Racecourse. Similarly, when Overseers of the Poor, Enclosure Commissioners, Turnpike Trustees and Surveyors of the Highways were appointed at local inns, innkeepers were often amongst those people chosen. They also played an important administrative role in the holding of inquests, the collection of rents, banking, the leasing of property, creditors' meetings and, as mentioned earlier, the quartering and recruiting of troops.

In conclusion, we can say that the innkeepers formed a worthy and enterprising section of the community. During the long wars with France they were unstintingly patriotic in raising funds for the defence of the country; they promoted many communal services and, whilst there must have been a substantial amount of self-interest and reward behind their enterprises, the contribution made by innkeepers towards the social and economic development of their communities was considerable. It is clear from newspaper notices that there was regular movement of innkeepers to new and better premises. Beerhouse keepers often aspired to become publicans, and publicans in their turn looked for promotion as innkeepers. Deservedly, they came to be recognised as a respectable and highly valued group within their community.

5. The Clientele

Men have always formed the majority of pub customers and, indeed, for very many years the presence of women in public houses was viewed with alarm and distaste. It was commonly felt that only women of a certain type would haunt the often rough, dirty and noisy alehouses. Even in the early twentieth century it would seldom occur to most women to go into a pub - a sentiment supported by the growth in popular opinion over the previous century that the woman's place was in the home. In the *Memoirs of John Holmes*, written in the mid nineteenth century, the author constantly refers to visiting local public houses, but only mentions the presence of women when they came to demand the return of their husband.[15] Attitudes to women visiting pubs did relax following the two world wars when many women had been drawn into the workforce for the first time in large numbers and began to assert their independence.

In literature, the most celebrated visit of a middle class woman to a Southwell inn, the *Saracen's Head*, comes in Nottinghamshire writer, DH Lawrence's *Women in Love*. Schoolmistress Ursula, in love with Birkin, is taken out in the car by him for the afternoon.

> *We'll have our high tea at the Saracen's Head, [he says].... She stood in the old yard of the inn, smelling of straw and stables and petrol. Above, she could see the first stars...They sat together in a little parlour by the fire... She looked at him. He still seemed so separate. New eyes were opened in her soul. She saw a strange creature from another world, in him. ... They laughed, and went to the meal provided. There was a venison pasty, of all things, a large broad-faced cut ham, eggs and cresses and red beet-root, and medlars and apple-tart, and tea.*

Yet this change in attitude to women frequenting public houses was only gradual; several women recalled to me that even in the 1950s the only time they went into a Southwell pub was when they were sent to collect a jug of beer from the pub hatch in the passageway. They never actually ventured into a room.

Whilst the majority of those who used Southwell's inns and alehouses in the eighteenth century were men from the labouring poor, the upper and middle classes, both men and women, were by no means absent from local inns. Their visits would have been as a result of travel or as participants in the wide range of economic and social activities centred there. Robert Hardstaff's *Georgian Diary* is full of references to George Hodgkinson's social group regularly visiting the *Crown*, *Cross Keys*, the *Castle* and the *Saracen's Head* for dinners and business meetings or for sporting occasions such as cock-fighting or prize fights.

Cock-fighting and wrestling were two popular activities that took place at local inns in the eighteenth century. All sports and games would have been considered suitable for a bet.

From the mid nineteenth century however, the available evidence suggests that the upper and middle classes were using local inns much less frequently. Why was this? By the 1840s the coaching trade had started its decline and local inns had begun to lose much of their economic and social importance. The most important reason for this change of attitude amongst the upper classes, however, may be due to the growing concern about drink. The increase in the number of licensed premises following the Beer Act of 1830 encouraged the activities of the Temperance Movement which aimed at establishing complete abstinence from alcoholic drink. This had an impact on the attitudes of the upper and middle classes by working to undermine the respectability of the public house.

For the great mass of the male working class labourers, however, the local public house spelled paradise. One particular group who would have enjoyed the King Street pubs would have been the carriers. Carrying services continued to be based at Southwell public houses until the end of the nineteenth century. As carriers would be constantly working in the innyards they would use the facilities not just for meal breaks but also for relaxing with a pint at the end of the day. Workers' organisations like friendly societies, trade unions and 'lodges' would also be based at local inns and public houses. We have firm evidence in the eighteenth and nineteenth centuries that friendly societies and other workers' organisations met regularly in private rooms at the *Wheatsheaf*, the *White Swan*, the *Black Bull* and the *Crown*. Added to this, the lodges of the Oddfellows and Foresters met in public houses in Easthorpe and Westhorpe. Regular clients at the *George and Dragon* and at the *Lord Nelson* recall upstairs rooms being referred to as the 'Buffs' Room (Lodge of Buffaloes).

R.A.O.B. GRAND COUNCIL
1309 Dragon Lodge, Southwell.   July, 1947

W. Hopewell, Senr.   W. Hopewell, Junr.   C. Martin.   J. Covell, C.P.   F. Scraton.   H. Hollis.   W. Charity.   J. W. Cobb, C.P.   T. Hobson, C.P.
F. Marshall, K.O.M.   W. Burton, C.P.   J. Whitworth.   W. Nettleship.   H. McGowan.   M. Jarvis, C.P.   C. E. Best, C.P.   H. Booth, K.O.M.
W. J. Cooper, C.P.   J. Irvine.   A. King, C.P.   A. Hall, C.P.   E. Wesley.   E. W. Ross, C.P.   A. Thompson.

The Royal Order of Buffaloes, a social and fraternal organisation founded in 1822, met for many years in Southwell public houses. This photograph is taken in front of the **George and Dragon** *in the 1950s. (Vincent Johnson-Cooper)*

Joseph Lawson, writing about Pudsey alehouses in the nineteenth century, considered the chief elements for a good night out in a local alehouse were *'talking, playing games and music'*.[15] John Holmes, in his references to Southwell public houses in the same period, seems to have a similar opinion. According to him sport, gambling and village gossip were favoured topics of conversation. As for pub games, there has always been a large variety, many activities taking place in the yards at the rear - quoits, skittles, blood sports and, of course, prize fighting. Several pub games have stood the test of time and are still with us today such as darts, cards, dominoes and billiards. In the *Memoirs* of John Holmes, the author comments that all sports and games in public houses were considered suitable for a bet.[16]

Music was the third of Joseph Lawson's essential pub activities. In the nineteenth century it was very common for regulars to sing songs of a traditional or romantic flavour. Landlords would give a free pint to the first man to start the singing, usually to the accompaniment of a piano or a fiddle.[17] Itinerant musicians often provided entertainment in their own right. My research has indicated that many pubs in the 1950s still kept to this tradition and there are people in Westhorpe to this day that have fond memories of evenings of music and informal singing at the *Lord Nelson* and the *Grapes*.

In conclusion, we can say that in the twenty-first century the 'local' remains central to many people's lives, but it does not attract the numbers it did a hundred or more years ago. Today potential clients, with a higher disposable income, have a much greater range of other leisure and sporting opportunities on which to spend their money. Furthermore, many organisations have their own facilities where they can meet and enjoy a social evening. Contributing further to the decline in pub attendance are the attractions of staying in the comfort of one's home, watching television whilst sampling cheap drink from the supermarket. The restrictions of the drink-drive and non-smoking laws deter some people from visiting a pub.

6. The Local Malting Industry

Stanley Chapman in *Southwell - The Town and its People Volume II* points out that, with the exception of textiles, *'malting was the most important industry of Southwell in the eighteenth and nineteenth century. In fact it was the premier industry of the whole of the Newark region.'* The barley used by maltsters was probably grown in the Southwell district, as were the hops needed by local brewers. Unfortunately we have only limited details of the numbers of town malting businesses in the late eighteenth century, but we can get a reasonable picture of the size of the industry from trade directories in the nineteenth century.

Maltsters operating in Southwell 1828 - 1892						
Year	King St.	Queen St.	Westgate	Burgage	Market Place	Total
1828	2	1	2	1	1	7
1832	3	1	2	1	1	8
1844	3	-	1	1	-	5
1853	3	-	1	1	1	6
1864	3	-	1	1	1	6
1872	2	-	1	1	1	5
1880	2	-	1	1	1	5
1892	1	-	-	-	-	1

It is noticeable that by the 1890s the trade was in decline, probably due to the strong competition from the larger maltings in Newark and Mansfield and the growth of factories in larger towns.

The Maltings on Lower Kirklington Road below Burgage Green, built in the 1820's. (Terry Pearce)

Where were the Southwell maltings?

We have evidence that a malthouse with a maltkiln was built below Burgage Green around 1825 by Charles Walker.[18] Walker was a brewer as well as a miller and landowner. The house signs of the 'Maltings' and the 'Old Brewmasters House', can still be clearly seen as you cross from the Burgage to Lower Kirklington Road. If you look carefully you will also be able to see the top of the old malt kiln, behind the main building.

*Bricked in windows, with a typical maltings style, in the wall along the Bramley Centre passageway. This could have been the location of the King Street domestic maltings, serving pubs like the **Portland Arms**, the **Admiral Rodney** and the **Black Bull**. (Terry Pearce)*

Another maltings – the Westgate maltings - was based next to Ealand's (Westgate) Brewery.[19] Brewery records inform us that in 1903 *'the brewery and maltings in Westgate were sold for £3,000'*. Twenty eight years later the brewery and maltings were sold for the last time before being demolished to make way for the Ideal Cinema. The location of the other three or four maltings is not so certain, although we can make educated guesses. A close study of the wall alongside the passageway next to Southwell Library, on King Street, shows bricked in windows, which have a typical maltings style about them. This domestic maltings would have probably served the *Black Bull* and *Portland Arms* and possibly the *Admiral Rodney*.

According to the trade directories there was also a domestic maltings close to the Old Market Place. This is supported by a newspaper notice from 1810 which refers to a malting office near the Market Place, with a kiln 16ft square, a working room 90ft x 20ft, a store room, *'a good steep vault capable of steeping the 14 quarters every fifth day'*.[20] In various directories from 1819 to 1835 the maltster's name was given as William Smith, which is the same name as the then innkeeper at the *Crown*. It may be reasonable to assume that the maltings were probably situated at the back of the inn. With regard to the maltings known to be located on or near Queen Street, a case can be made that an existing building, visible from the car park at the *Saracen's Head*, looks suspiciously like a former malting office. The design and size of the original windows would suggest this.

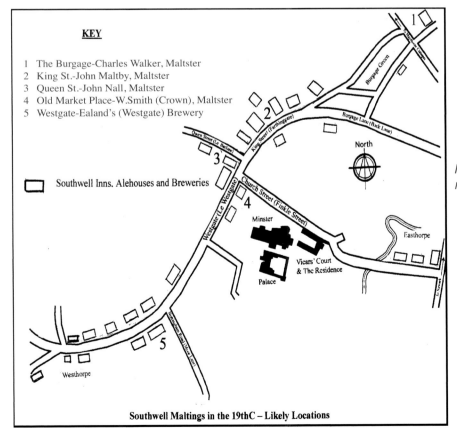

KEY

1 The Burgage-Charles Walker, Maltster
2 King St.-John Maltby, Maltster
3 Queen St.-John Nall, Maltster
4 Old Market Place-W.Smith (Crown), Maltster
5 Westgate-Ealand's (Westgate) Brewery

☐ Southwell Inns. Alehouses and Breweries

Southwell Maltings in the 19thC – Likely Locations

Map showing the possible location of maltings in Southwell

7. Local Opposition to the Drink Trade

From the 1780s an increase of religious fervour on a national scale led to a hardening of official attitudes to the drink trade, drunkenness and the large numbers of inns and alehouses. By the 1830s Southwell had over twenty five inns and beerhouses and yet its population was only c.2,000. We see this hardening of official attitudes in the way that Nottingham and Newark magistrates began to revoke more licences and restrict the numbers of new licences to innkeepers.

This change of attitude by the authorities to the drink trade was to some extent influenced by the Temperance Movement, with its twin aims of achieving legislation to ban the public sale of alcohol and persuading people to 'pledge' against the demon drink. The Temperance Movement was a response to the very real and serious social ills resulting from working men drinking away their wages, and the rise in domestic violence, poverty and destitution.

In 1823 the Revd. JT Becher, of Southwell, in his *Rules and Regulations of Southwell Friendly Institution*, insisted that *'Foresight, habitual Temperance and early Industry, can never be too forcibly impressed on the minds of the laborious Classes-DEATH is the punishment imposed upon wilful Transgression. Let it however be remembered, that the Sting of Death is Sin'*.

Temperance Society poster advertising a society excursion in 1872, an example of efforts to draw men away from the public houses

We get another glimpse of the Temperance issue some years later in the 1860s. In the *Reminiscences of Richard Fisher* the author recounts how the Salvation Army attempted to make converts in Southwell:

> *The Salvation Army tried to get started at Southwell. Mother had the two organisers to tea on Sunday. Old Harry joined them and was their drummer in the band; they marched up the street with their tambourines playing and Harry beating the drum.*
> *Harry backslided and got drunk one day; then brought out the drum and was beating up and down the street in front of his home until his wife got him inside. I saw him beating his drum.*
> *That finished the army's attempt to convert Southwell.*[21]

Thirty years later the author of *Our Nottinghamshire Villages* (1894) made a strong outburst against the numbers of public houses, especially in Southwell.

> *Our Village Public-Houses urgently demand attention.*
> *It is not a sin to make, to drink, or to sell intoxicating liquors; but alas a terrible band of army-followers run in the train of the drinking habits...in the shape of intemperance, blasted hopes, blighted characters, wife-beatings, starving children, assaults, murders, disease, pauperism, insanity...involving heavy burdens upon families, the parish and the state. And these ills are such that society is justified...in regulating, controlling and even by...suppressing the liquor trade...*
> *The number of public-houses is much too great. One to a thousand population would suffice.*
> *West Bridgeford thrives with four thousand people to one public-house...*
> *But the number in the Nottingham Petty Sessional division is one to each 278 inhabitants; while in the Southwell division it is one to each 147.*

Beware of intemperance . be

Beware of intemperance . be

Beware of intemperance . be

Beware of intemperance . be

Beware of intemperance . be

Beware of intemperance . be

Beware of intemperance . be

Beware of intemperance . be

William B. Gravell, May 4th.

A handwriting exercise on 'Intemperance', dating back to the 1860s, found recently at the Minster School.

There is more evidence of the local Temperance movement in Newark. Despite the town's reputation as a major malting and brewing town, the movement did make an impact. The Ossington Coffee Palace and Hotel was established in 1882 and this was followed by the founding of a local Band of Hope group, (the Temperance Youth Movement), in 1900.

That this adverse publicity had an effect on the business of Southwell publicans is suggested by two pieces of important evidence. Firstly, from the 1892 *Royal Commission Report on Rural Labour* we learn that the traditionally close ties between Friendly Societies and local public houses had loosened and that many working class labourers were members of other societies such as the Odd Fellows which were strongly linked to the Temperance Movement. The fact that clubrooms for local friendly and benefit societies were by the late 1800s no longer wholly centred on Southwell inns must have had some serious impact on publicans' trade. Secondly, for the period 1880-1920 the *Annual Southwell Brewster Sessions* regularly note that there were too many licensed premises by head of population (in 1897 one to every 144 inhabitants). Inevitably this hardening of attitudes towards the drink trade led to a refusal by magistrates to renew some licences. In 1908 and 1921 the applications by publicans from the *Black Bull* and the *White Swan* were both refused and consequently both public houses closed.

The Ossington Coffee Palace (c.1890).

Newark's Ossington Coffee Palace, a fine monument to the Temperance Movement. The hotel included a library, billiards room and assembly rooms as well as a coffee bar.

8. Lost inns, alehouses and breweries

Bar Lane Beerhouse

This beerhouse is recorded in the 1830s as being in Bar Lane,[22] now known as Queen Street, but the exact location is unknown. Almost certainly the beerhouse was opened as a result of the 1830 Beerhouse Act, which abolished the duty on beer and established the right of any householder to sell beer upon purchase of a two guinea licence from the Excise Office. With the price of beer halved overnight, the number of beerhouses soared all over the country. Unfortunately we have little knowledge of the Bar Lane beerhouse other than the beerkeeper throughout the 1830s was Adam Cooke.

Bear

We have little information on this public house except for two references from the *Nottingham Journal* in 1784 and 1786. We do know that it was situated in Westgate but we have no precise location. The only detail provided by the newspapers is that the *Bear* was next to some maltkilns and malt offices.

> *N J - October 2 1784* **To Be LET**
> *And entered upon immediately All that good accustomed Public House, known by the Sign of the BEAR, situate standing and being in Southwell. Also the Maltkilns and Malt Offices thereby adjoining. Further particulars apply to Mr William Wier, now Resident on the premises.*

Two years later the same newspaper, on February 18th, reports that the *Bear* is to be sold along with *'Malt Office ...with Homestead adjoining, containing nearly one acre, planted with fruit trees.'*

Name. The *Bear* was a common name for an inn or alehouse in less enlightened times when bear baiting and bear whipping were popular entertainments. However, there might be a more interesting explanation for its name. Mary West unearthed evidence from the *Patent Rolls* (1549) that in Westhorpe, *'Lands and Liberties here went with the lordship and manor of Southwell to John, Earl of Warwick.'* As the bear and ragged staff came to be used from the sixteenth century by the Earls of Warwick as part of their coat of arms, might this explain why the alehouse came to be called the *Bear?* In Newark Market Place there can still be seen a post for bears to be chained to before they gave the crowds the vulgar entertainment they had come to witness. We have no direct evidence of bear baiting in Southwell.

Black Bull

Situation. The *Black Bull* was situated in King Street, first in a line of public houses on that street ending with the *White Swan*. After its closure in 1909 it became a shop as did most of its outbuildings in Bull Yard. For many years it was Benet's Clothing shop and is now occupied by Elizabeth Jane, a womens' clothing shop. The sign for Bull Yard still remains and as you make your way from King Street into Bull Yard you get a strong feeling that a substantial inn once occupied the premises. The significance of the inn name is that the bull was an heraldic symbol in the coat of arms of the Duke of York, one of the most powerful families in the country.

Description. An *Inventory (1908)* indicates that at the front of the inn there was a *'Bar, Tap Room, Bar Parlour (with a piano) and Club Room. Accommodation for travellers was provided by 5 bedrooms, stabling for 8 horses'*.[23] A much earlier deed (1765-81) refers as well to *'dwelling houses, stabling, yards, gardens, backsides, outbuildings with a passage for carter and carriages leading to the yard'*.[24] In addition to these buildings and open spaces the old inn possessed its own brewhouse. An excellent piece of evidence showing how lively the scene would have been around the *Black Bull* comes from a *Nottingham Journal* advertisement in 1782.

*A photograph of the **Black Bull** just before its closure in 1909. (NA PS/B 10/1)*

Commercial activities. Evidence, especially from contemporary local newpapers, indicates that the *Black Bull* was one of the earliest of the Southwell inns to profit by the commercial benefits that improvements in transport and roads created. This *Nottingham Journal* notice of 1769 illustrates the point. *'Post Chaise for Hire — A genteel Post Chaise with able horses may be had on short notice, to travel from Southwell to Newark, Nottingham and Mansfield at Mr.George Botham's Black Bull in Southwell, conducted by a careful driver'.*

Much business would have come the way of the *Black Bull* from being a carrier base. Trade Directories show that village carriers from all over the region brought their waggons into the yards of inns like the *Black Bull* on a daily basis and the ensuing trade would have provided an extra source of income for the innkeeper. A profitable business was also done in horse breeding as the following newspaper advertisement shows.

M A R T I N,
GROCER, CHANDLER, SOAP BOILER, FLAX-DRESSER, and ROPE-MAKER,
S O U T H W E L L :

TAKES this Mode of acquainting his Friends, and the Public in general, that he has purchased Part of the Black Bull Inn, Southwell aforefaid ; where he intends carrying on the feveral Branches of his Profeffion, and humbly folicits their Countenance.

Thofe who pleafe to honour him with their Commands, may depend on being ferved in the beft Manner, and their Favours ever gratefully acknowledged.

₀ J. MARTIN can only deal in the Chandlery and Soap Bufinefs till the 1ft of March next ; when he flatters himfelt his Shop will be fitted up in a complete Manner.

This notice from 1782 gives an excellent idea of how commercially active inn yards would have been at this time. Many trades would sell their wares there. (NJ Dec. 28 1782)

> *NJ - April 21 1770* **Stud Breeding**
> *To Cover this Season—— at Mr.Botham's Black Bull At Half a Guinea — the Mare and One Shilling – the Servant* **LIBERTY** *The first season of her covering. A beautiful high bred Brown Bay Colt, the property of Mr Lowe of Farnsfield.*

As well as the commercial activity that clearly existed at the inn, successive landlords worked at establishing the *Black Bull* as an attractive venue for the professional classes. The local lawyer, George Hodgkinson, dined there in 1781 with his social set and his father used the *Black Bull* as the base for his Enclosure meetings, as reported in the *Nottingham Journal* on February 29 1772. *'At the Black Bull – To consider further the reasons for enclosing the Commons (Cotmoor, Radley) All interested are asked to attend.'*

Innkeepers. In the mid eighteenth century, the *Black Bull* was kept by a very well known local figure, William Botham, who had established a strong reputation as a highly successful entrepreneur. The *Nottingham Journal* is full of advertisements covering sales, auctions, horse breeding, the post chaise business and various meetings all centred on the *Black Bull* during his time. The last entry in the journal about William Botham is where he says farewell to his former clients.

> *NJ – May 20 1775* **William Botham**
> *Who lately kept the Black Bull gives thanks to his Friends and Customers for all the favours they confer on him and begs leave to acquaint the Nobility and Gentry and others that he is removed to the Red Lion Inn, Worksop which he has fitted up in a genteel and elegant manner and that hath laid a fresh stock of wines and other liquors and provided a good Post Chaise, able Horses and careful drivers to be ready on the shortest notice to travel to any part of England and he further begs leave to allure all those who may be pleased to honour him.*
> *By their most obedient and humble servant William Botham.*

Several of William Botham's successors as innkeeper had other occupations - a very common practice in the nineteenth century. Richard Rawson was a maltster, clearly closely linked to his main job. On the other hand Henry Dixon in 1881 appeared in the census as a sanitary inspector –not so easy to see a link here. As with other town inns it was quite common for husband and wife to work as a team. One particular partnership that stood out at the *Black Bull* was the team of William and Martha Bradley, who ran the inn from c.1850-1870.

Successive innkeepers brewed their own beer on the premises until the late nineteenth century, but by that time it had become uneconomic for innkeepers to continue this practice and in its final years the *Black Bull* was tied to the Warwick and Richardson Brewery at Newark.

Closure. Despite the fact that the *Black Bull* had been one of the town's most successful carrier inns it faced closure in 1909. The magistrates' attitude to the drink trade seemed by this time to have been hardened by a number of factors, including the criticisms of the Temperance Movement. We see this change in attitude in the stricter control over the granting of licences to innkeepers. As the following licensing record shows there was no evidence given to the magistrates to indicate that the *Black Bull* had a bad reputation for drunkenness on their premises. It seems that the main reason for not renewing the licence was that there were too many public houses, particularly in King Street.

> **Southwell Petty Sessions** *March 13 1908* **Annual Licensing Meeting**
> *That having regard to the character ....and the number of licensed houses in the immediate vicinity, the licence of the Black Bull is unnecessary.*

> **Evidence   Henry Sills, Superintendent of Police**
> *There are 7 fully licensed premises within 300 yards of the Black Bull and also 5 off licenses. The population of Southwell was 3161 in 1901- with 15 on licenses and 14 fully licensed, plus 1 beerhouse and 7 off licenses. This gives 1 licensed premise to 143 of the population. In my judgement this license is not required as the number of licensed premises on King St is excessive. As regards Police Supervision there is no entrance to the Black Bull Inn from King St. The only entry is 12 yards down the passage. This passage extends to a yard which extends 110 yards into Queen St.. As there are another six properties in the yard, the yard is not under the control of... the Black Bull. This makes policing more difficult. I do not suggest the Black Bull has been used by the licensee improperly. Mr Foster is one of the oldest innkeepers in Southwell. He has kept the Black Bull in an exemplary manner.*

Black Horse

Situation. This beerhouse was situated in Back Lane, now Burgage Lane. Although we have no detail about its exact location it is reasonable to believe it would have been towards the top of the lane, near the junction with Farthing Street (King Street) because of the presence of large residences further down the lane. The *Black Horse* almost certainly would have come into existence as a result of the Beerhouse Act of 1830 and would have only been permitted to sell beer as the licence would not have extended to wine or spirits.

Limited evidence. Pigot's Directory of 1841-2 that tells us that the keeper at the *Black Horse* was Joseph Stanfield, who had been there since at least 1832. We have no exact knowledge as to how long the *Black Horse* stayed open, but it seems likely that it had closed by the 1870s.

Boot and Shoe

Situation. This old alehouse was situated on the Burgage but we are given no precise information as to exactly where. It could have been located at the lower end of the Burgage, close to the junction with Station Road and Lower Kirklington Road. There were a number of maltings in the town in the eighteenth and nineteenth centuries, one of which was situated close to that junction, opposite the old House of Correction. This building still stands today and is known as The Maltings. An alternative location for the *Boot and Shoe* could have been on the left hand side of the road as you approach the War Memorial from the Burgage crossroads where there were likely to have been a number of cottages.

> **To be SOLD by Private Contract,**
> A Small FREEHOLD ESTATE, fituate at Burrage, in the Parish of Southwell, and County of Nottingham, known by the Sign of the BOOT and SHOE, confifting of a Dwelling Houfe, Brewhoufe, Coal-houfe, and Stable, with Yard, Garden, and Orchard.
> For further Particulars apply to Mr. WILLIAM ADAMS, Jun. at Southwell.

*Notice of the sale of the **Boot and Shoe** in 1783. Where was it located?*
(NJ May 3 1783)

Limited evidence. The only evidence we have about the *Boot and Shoe* comes from a For Sale notice in the *Nottingham Journal* in 1783. From the description it appears slightly larger in size than most alehouses of the eighteenth century [25]. The Burgage was being gentrified at this period by the clearance of cottages and the building of the grand houses that now dominate it.

Name. The boot is a very common inn sign. There would have been several cobblers in Southwell and it is possible the premises would have been at one time occupied by shoemakers. Cobblers also had a 'thirsty' reputation so it is just possible the sign might have originated from that tradition.

Castle

Situation. The *Castle* was situated on Westgate by the west entrance to the Minster. An 1802 Survey provides evidence of this. *'In the Occupation of Hugh Maltby - A Public House, known by the Sign of the CASTLE and Yard in the town of Southwell, the Church Yard North, the Street South and lane leading to the Church Yard East and a house belonging to a Mr. West'.* [26]

It would seem likely from studying the print of 1814 and the *Nottingham Journal* that the *Castle* opened as an inn in the early 1700s and by the end of the eighteenth century had become one of the town's most prominent inns. However in the early 1820s the building was demolished, leaving us today with an excellent view of Southwell Minster from Westgate.

There is no precise evidence to explain why the *Castle* was demolished, but it seems likely that the large inn protruded into Westgate and might have caused a problem for the increasing coaching traffic. Another factor behind the

The *Castle* Inn is on the right. This view is taken from the churchyard, looking to Westgate.
(The Beauties of England and Wales, 1814).

decision was the idea to demolish the Chauntry House and other buildings around the west entrance to the Minster to build a new Grammar School, as Richard Ingleman's plan of 1819 shows. The 1819 plan and the 1814 print indicate that the inn was of some size and, in addition to the traditional layout of Tap Room and Parlour on the ground floor, it would have provided accommodation upstairs for travellers. Its proximity to the Minster would have been extremely convenient for pilgrims, religious groups and other visitors. In addition the inn possessed a substantial yard and stables that would be vital for its commercial life.

In the absence of specialist auction rooms in the town, many of Southwell's more prominent inns did a profitable business in the selling of property. The *Nottingham Journal* reported that on the 8th May 1773 *'At the Sign of the Castle, in the possession of Mr. Blundell - a Freehold Estate for sale - Norwood Field, Halam in the possession of Mr. C Sturtevant'.*

Clientele. They included George Hodgkinson's social set, who regularly met at the more upmarket town inns. George Hodgkinson's diary for the 13th January, 1781 states *'Court Day at Nicholson's (Castle Inn) .....Dined at the Court. Mr. Stenton was with me. No business. The jury went to take a view of some lands at Upton.'*

This extract also shows how important some town inns were in providing facilities for groups of people involved in local administration. The *Castle* Inn would have been convenient for those attending court at the Archbishop of York's Palace, a mere stone's throw away. On June 8, 1781, Hodgkinson continues *'Drank tea with Mrs. Stenton and adjourned in the evening to Nicholson's (Castle Inn) – he having an excellent tap of ale.'*

Innkeepers. We have evidence that Mr. Blundell was in post in 1773. Eight years later, in 1781 the innkeeper was Mr. Nicholson, followed by in 1791 Thomas Collinson. Finally, a few years before its demolition the innkeeper was Hugh Maltby.

Name. The *Castle* was a popular name for an inn sign as castles were a prominent feature of the landscape in most counties. There is no strong evidence, however, that Southwell ever had a castle.

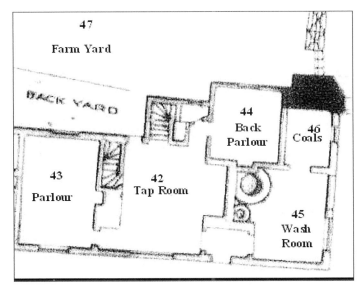

Architect Richard Ingleman's plan of 1819. He also designed the later House of Correction in 1807 and the Assembly Rooms two years earlier.

Cross Keys

Situation. The *Cross Keys* Inn dated back to the early 1700s and was situated in the Old Market Place, next to the junction of Bar Lane (Queen Street) and Farthing Gate (King Street). The following notice from the *Nottingham Journal* on the 1st May 1790 provides some evidence for this location. *'To Be Let and entered upon immediately. The Old Cross Keys, situate in the Market Place. Further particulars - see Mr.B.Cadsby on the premises'.*

Commercial importance. The *Cross Keys* was one of the town's most commercially active inns in the eighteenth century. It also attracted the higher class of clientele as the *Georgian Diary (1781)* of George Hodgkinson showed. Its popularity was not solely due to its central position in the town. It was clearly a substantial property and as an inn it would have had a number of rooms for accommodating travellers. It also possessed a brewhouse, stables, yard, offices and outbuildings. This newspaper entry provides some useful background information.

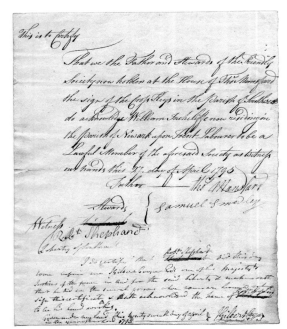

1795 Friendly Society membership certificate for a labourer, William Incliffle. This society met at the **Cross Keys** for their meetings.
(NA C/Q/DC 3/6)

> *NJ –Feb. 2 1788 Cross Keys Inn – To Be Sold*
> *All that good accustomed Inn, situate at Southwell, conveniently known by the name of the Cross Keys together with Brewhouse, Stables and other Out Offices belonging. And also a very convenient croft and homestead adjoining in the occupation of John Frith. Apply to Mr. J Aldridge.*

In the period before 1800 no other Southwell inn, with the exception of the *Saracen's Head,* did so much business in sales and auctions as the *Cross Keys*. The following entry in the *Nottingham Journal* on April 15 1769 illustrates the point. *'To be Sold At the house of William Cade, being the Cross Keys in Southwell ... A Freehold Estate at Normanton.'*

Local church and professional groups used the *Cross Keys* regularly for meetings as this newspaper entry shows. June 15 1774 *'Meeting at Cross Keys - of contributors to the relief of distressed families of clergy within the Archdeaconry – here the treasury accounts will be audited'.*

George Hodgkinson, in his 1781 diary, clearly sees the *Cross Keys* as his favourite town inn, judging from the number of occasions he and his social set dined or drank there. Some of his visits would have had a professional purpose, as on the 6th June 1781 when he *'Adjourned to Cade's where I drew up a bond from Mr.William Taylor of Kneesall to Mrs.E. Franks for £50'.*

But most visits that George Hodgkinson made to the *Cross Keys* were undoubtedly to enjoy the 'excellent ale' along with his social set, usually members of the Becher, Lowe, Stenton and Clay families. The following diary entry illustrates this. *20 February 1781 'Adjourned to our Oyster Club at Cade's but no oysters arrived.'* Again the quality of the ale at the *Cross Keys* is good cause for comment in the following diary entry. *8 March 1781 'Dined at the Pig Feast, at Cade's which is an annual treat - he treated us with an excellent good dinner, excellent port and capital punch.'*

Innkeepers. We have limited knowledge of the innkeepers, other than the generous tributes given by George Hodgkinson to the way William Cade kept his ale. Cade was followed by John Frith and then in 1788 Thomas Mansford, who is also recorded as being landlord of the *Wheatsheaf,* took over. A deed from 1786 throws some light on the transfer of the property.

> **Sale of *Cross Keys Inn*, June 1786**
> *This INDENTURE made the 22nd June in the twentieth year of our sovereign Lord, George the Third (King of England) ...between Edward Caunt of Nottingham and John Frith of Southwell - whereas John Frith has contracted with Mary Fowler for the purchase of the messauge and premises for the price of £495, the property commonly known by the Sign of the Cross Keys, late in the occupation of William Cade and now of the said John Frith with the croft and orchard, together with all outhouses buildings, barns, stables, yards and gardens. (NA DD/M 71/452)*

Name. The *Cross Keys* was a popular name for an inn. The *Cross Keys* were the arms of the Papal See, the emblem of St.Peter and his successors. The sign was frequently adopted by innkeepers and tenants of religious houses and it is quite possible that, being an inn, the *Cross Keys* would have provided accommodation for a good many religious visitors, possibly even pilgrims, to Southwell Minster.

Demolition. We have no definite evidence as to why the *Cross Keys* was demolished but we do know that as a result of the road linking Mansfield and Leadenham becoming a turnpike, the carrier and coaching trade through Southwell increased greatly. The coaches and waggons would have found the entrance at the junction of Bar Lane (Queen Street) and Farthing Gate (King Street) extremely narrow and consequently commercial pressures may have been applied to have the *Cross Keys* demolished.

*A photograph of the **Grapes** in the early twentieth century. Note the brewery name on the wall, much clearer than today. (Southwell Civic Society.)*

Grapes

Situation. The *Grapes*, also known as the *Bricklayer's Arms*, was situated in Westhorpe on the corner of Allenby Road and Westhorpe. It is now Ralph Downing's Antique shop. It opened as a beerhouse just after the 1830 Beerhouse Act. The *Grapes* closed in 1974/5.

Description. Looking at the former beerhouse today you can see that the front of the building is more recent than the rear. Further back, in the old Tap room and Public Bar, there are old timber beams that suggest the main part of the building is at least 250 years old. Yvonne and Harry Cooling remember the bar being very cosy, with a welcoming open fire and four or five small tables with chairs. The nearby Tap Room had benches along one wall and a large picture of the Warwick and Richardson Brewery coat of arms. Upstairs the *Grapes* had a spacious room that was in earlier years regularly used by both private and community groups based in Westhorpe. Outside, at the front, there was a sweet shop and, at the back, a range of outbuildings on the corner, including Foster's blacksmith's shop. These were demolished in 1930 when the main Oxton Road was widened. Also, like many public houses, the *Grapes* had a large garden, extending very nearly to Halam Road, where poultry and pigs were kept. In addition there were allotments and a large orchard –all contributing extra sources of income for the landlord.

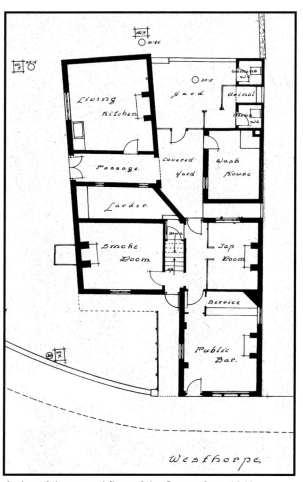

A plan of the ground floor of the Grapes from 1949.
(NA PS/B 27/22)

Memories. Elderly people in the Westhorpe community remember the pub fondly as having a very homely, welcoming character. Yvonne and Harry Cooling remember the bar and tap rooms being frequented by local working men, a number of whom were employed at Ransome and Marles at Newark and who talked a lot of 'shop'. They would gather in front of the open fire in the bar and play dominoes, darts and table skittles. Arthur Frecknall, the last landlord, told me it was quite common for there to be queues of local working men waiting for him to open up so they could get their preferred chair and table by the fire and then 'on with the game'. There were some real characters in the *Grapes* at this time, such as 'Dickie' Ducker, who lodged in the Sunnyside Cottages. Yvonne Cooling told me 'Dickie' was a Sherwood Forester and he would regularly arrange a bus trip to Crich to attend the annual Memorial Service. Few women would be seen in the Bar or Tap Room. However it was quite common for couples to go into the Smoke Room, where there was a piano and 'sing-songs' took place. Roland Cottam of Landseer Road would often lead the way and on some occasions the White Heather Club performed. At the side of the *Grapes* the landlords, for many years, had a sweet shop where ice cream was also sold. At the back was the large garden where Arthur Frecknall kept 400 poultry and some pigs. In later years the room upstairs was not used but in earlier times it had been used regularly by the people of Westhorpe and other community groups. The following article from a local newspaper in October 1869 illustrates this point:

> *Nottingham Review - October 1st 1869* **The Thorn Tea**
> *Southwell – A few evening ago a social gathering took place at Mr.John Knight's, the Grapes in Westhorpe, when about 120 sat down to an excellent tea, served up in good style by the worthy host. The affair originated somewhat curiously a year ago, and was called the Thorn Tea and it is intended to celebrate it annually. It appears ...that a farmer sold a quantity of thorns to a neighbour, and there being some dispute respecting the price charged, the money received was handed over to Mr.Knight to provide tea for a number of poor people, residents' of Westhorpe; several asked to contribute a small sum, and as it was a jovial affair they have again subscribed until it has reached a considerable affair. All greatly enjoyed themselves, and after tea, dancing was kept up till eleven o'clock, when each and all returned home, wishing to be again present at the annual Thorn Tea Party.*

In more recent times local sports teams frequented the *Grapes* for their meetings, particularly Westhorpe Cricket teams. During the two world wars, troops stationed at Norwood Park certainly spent a lot of their spare time at the pub. In earlier times agricultural workers and framework knitters were among the regular clientele, many of whom lived in the Westhorpe area. Less regular customers in later years would be coach travellers bound for the east coast or for Southwell Racecourse. According to Arthur and Eva Frecknall the custom was for the coach drivers to stop by the *Nelson* and the *Grapes* and for the travellers to call in for a break at either public house or both!

Beerhouse keepers. The first beerhouse keeper was Samuel Hibbert, a gardener, who bought the property, which included an orchard and brick kiln, in 1820 from a Mr.William Thompson for £200. Samuel and Sarah Hibbert ran the *Grapes* from 1830 – 68. They were followed in 1868 by another beerhouse keeper with an additional occupation, Nathaniel Parkin, who was a builder.

The following year Nathaniel Parkin caused a major scandal as this local newspaper article illustrates:

Nottingham Review-Sept. 10th 1869 **Murderous Assault by a Beerhouse Keeper**
An assault of a most dangerous nature was committed at Southwell
on Saturday afternoon, which at the time was thought fatal.
At Westhorpe there is a beerhouse (the Grapes) now kept by the chief actor in the scene, Nathaniel
Parkin, who stands committed to take his trial...to be holden at Newark.
It appears that two youths went into the beerhouse and called for a pint of ale, one of them a sweep,
about seventeen years of age, asking Parkin for twopence, which he alleged was owing to him for
sweeping a chimney. An altercation ensued and the youth and Parkin had further words, and at last the
sweep said if he could not have the money out of Parkin's pocket he would take it out of his hide, using
very abusive and threatening language.
Parkin returned to the house, and took up a poker, with which he went into the yard,
and struck the youth a severe blow on the back of his head, laying the skull open.
The police were at once communicated with and a surgeon fetched;
the former apprehending Parkin and the latter attending to the injury inflicted
and under the able treatment of Dr.Elliott
the youth is progressing as favourably as expected.

The 'infamous' Mr.Parkin was followed by Thomas Richmond, who was also a basketmaker. It was necessary for many beerhouse keepers to have another job to supplement their income and the next two people were examples of this trend. Thomas Richmond was shown in the 1881 census to be a basketmaker and he was followed as beerhouse keeper by Thomas Dodd, a painter and decorator. In 1887 Dodd, too, hit the headlines when, after a meeting at the *Grapes*, he was declared bankrupt.

Nottingham Weekly Express - Nov. 4th 1887 **Failure of a Beerhouse Keeper**
Report of a meeting *of the creditors of John Henry Dodd of the Grapes Inn, Southwell.*
The debtor's liabilities £402. 17s. 7d expected ...dividend £360. 6s. 5d
Less: preferred creditors for rents, rates etc ...Deficiency £345.5s.11d ...
The Causes of failure were inability to meet pressure from creditors and want of capital.
The Official Receiver said: 'The Debtor commenced business as a painter about nine years ago
without capital... A little over four years ago he entered the Grapes Inn.
His statement of affairs shows a deficiency of £345. 5s. 11d
The debtor had a house left to him by his father subject to the payment of £100 to his brothers and
sisters which property is stated by the debtor to be worth less than the morgage money and interest due
thereon. Should the preferential items hold good there can be little for creditors.
The debtor has no offer to make.
There was no creditor present... the debtor has been adjudicated a bankrupt...

Many local Westhorpe people remember fondly the last landlord and his wife, Arthur and Eva Frecknall. They ran the house from 1953 to its closure in 1974. They later took a public house at Edingley and then retired to Laxton where I visited them. Arthur Frecknall told me he had only been married one week before he began running the *Grapes*. He pointed out to me that the brewery had only just put pumps into the *Grapes* a short time before he came in. Landlords had been in the habit of bringing the beer up from the cellar in large jugs. Also interesting is that the *Grapes* had only applied for a spirits licence in the late 1940s. When I asked Arthur if he remembered the prices of beer in 1953 he immediately replied, using old money terms, '*10d Mild, 11d Bitter, 15d Spirits*'.

From the end of the nineteenth century the *Grapes* ceased to brew its own beer. It became tied to the W.S.Davy's Brewery, Newark, which was taken over by Warwick and Richardson Brewery, also of Newark, in 1920. It is still possible to see the brewery lettering faintly on the side of the building as you approach from the Oxton Road.

Closure. The *Grapes* closed in 1975 to the regret of many local Westhorpe people. John Smith's Brewery had taken over from Warwick and Richardson and then John Smith's itself was taken over by Courage. Courage, in 1975, no doubt conscious of the refurbishing of the *Nelson* opposite, decided on a policy of reducing the numbers of its tied houses and this resulted in the closure of both the *Grapes* and their other Southwell house, the *Shoulder of Mutton*.

King Street Beerhouse

Whilst we know there was a beerhouse in King Street from 1830 to around 1860 we cannot be sure exactly where it was located. Like several others in the town this one would have opened after the 1830 Beerhouse Act.

Beerhouse keeper. The first beerhouse keeper is listed as William Jallings who was also referred to in the trade directories as a butcher.[27] Trade Directories after 1860 make no mention of the beerhouse so it is reasonable to assume it had been closed at some time in the 1850s.

*The **Portland Arms** for many years was adjacent to Simpkins' Garage. Many of the workers there were amongst the regular clients. (Nottinghamshire County Council - Southwell Library)*

Portland Arms

Situation. This public house, affectionately known in its last years as the 'Devil's Kitchen', was sited in King Street where the Portland Arcade stands today. In 1969 the pub was closed and replaced soon afterwards with a small group of shops.

It is likely that an alehouse was located on this site in the early 1700s. Structural alterations took place over the years and the present facade probably dates to around 1900. There is a 1790 deed, at a time when the Horsley family ran the *Portland Arms,* that suggests the property was of some size with *'barn, stable outhouses and brewhouse'.* [28] In some trade directories in the early 1800s it was known as the *Rutland Arms.* As with other town inns, the *Portland Arms* had the outside space and rooms to run sales and auctions of all descriptions. The following example from 1861 of the sale of a prominent Southwell windmill, illustrates the point.

The *Portland Arms* would have used its yard, stable and outbuildings for the carrier trade. Village carriers would have brought their waggons full of produce to the yard, market stalls were set up and regular commerce with local people would have taken place.

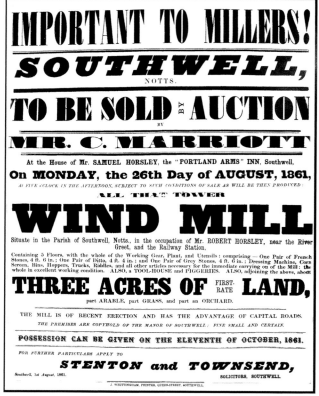

*The **Portland Arms** regularly held auctions such as this one in 1861 of a Tower Windmill which was located near the Railway Station and the River Greet. (NA DD/M 71/231/2)*

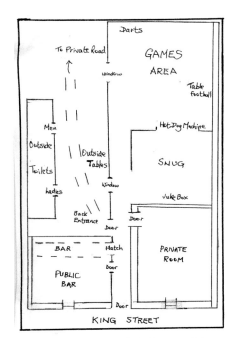

An approximate plan of the layout of the Portland Arms just before closure.

Description. Several local people vividly recall the layout of rooms as they existed in the 1950s and 1960s. Joan Nix remembers entering the building from King Street and turning left to go into the Public Bar. There were benches round the edge of the room and many people also sat at tables in the middle, playing either cards or dominoes. Further down the passageway were two other rooms; the first, on the right, had a juke-box and consequently usually attracted a group of younger people. The back room housed the legendary hot dog machine and it was in here that table football and darts were played. In the yard outside, on the way to Private Road from the arcade, were the toilet block on the left and a sitting area with tables on the right. According to Herbert Lewin there was a room on the first floor of one of the outhouses to the right, which the landlords opened up to the unemployed. For a short time in the 1950s when Herbert was out of work he used to go there and play dominoes and cards for matchsticks. The old cellars, which are very extensive, can still be visited today.

Wartime and post-war memories. 'Jock' Grant first visited the *Portland Arms* just before the Second World War broke out. He recalls the landlord, an ex-policeman called Henry Forman, kept a cockatoo that was particularly vicious. In the war years 'Jock' remembers the pub as being a favourite haunt of the French Canadian soldiers camped on the edge of town near Norwood Park. To many people it was very much a pub that appealed to the younger generation. Joan Nix recalls how groups of 'bikers', including herself and fellow bikers from Southwell, Mansfield, Rainworth and Newark would meet on their motorcycles at the Westhorpe crossroads. They would buy some fish and chips from the shop there and move through the town on their bikes to the *Portland Arms*.

The favourite area in the pub for many of the younger generation was at the back where there was a juke box and the famous hotdog machine. Dennis Broomfield , Vincent Johnson-Cooper and Roland Towers never saw any machine quite like this one. It had a series of spikes rising from the base. The landlord, John Crepeau, would force the bread cob onto the spike and then drop the long, delicious sausage into the cob. Adding mushy peas and tomato sauce would complete the job. Amongst the regulars Dennis 'Toothache' Johnson is remembered as a character. He liked his ale and usually had a lot to say on any subject. He fought in the Korean War and in later years he worked at Rainbows Transport. The *Portland Arms* was also a favourite port of call for the Southwell Motor Company. Herbert Lewin recalls that as a young boy working at Merryweathers on Halam Road he would be expected by his workmates, at lunchtime, to run down to the *Portland Arms* and bring back a big jug of ale.

Landlords. The Horsley family ran the public house for a very long time, from 1790 to 1883. Samuel Horsley Senior was a hopgrower in addition to being landlord and his son, Samuel Horsley Junior, was a grocer. Landlords having a second occupation was a common practice in the town and especially at the *Portland Arms*. Two other landlords had multiple occupations – trade directories indicate that Frank Wilkins was also a farmer in 1885 and 'Fred' Denman was a brazier and tinner in 1891.

We know more about the last landlord of the *Portland Arms*, John Crepeau. By nationality a French Canadian, John Crepeau had lived in the USA and France before coming to England in 1937. Herbert Lewin recalls how John would allow regulars who were short of cash to put what they owed 'on the slate' until Friday. John Crepeau would stand no nonsense but he had a good sense of humour. When the *Saracen's Head* made it quite plain that they would not tolerate anyone going into their hotel in muddy boots he placed a big poster

John Crepeau, the last landlord of the Portland Arms, in 1969. (Newark Advertiser)

at the entrance stating *'Farmers and Labourers welcome! Boots and All!'* John Crepeau joined the Royal Army Service Corps and had a distinguished war record, as the following extract from the *Newark Advertiser* on December 27th 1969 shows.

Young men, and some not so young have always found it a challenge that there are 13 hotels and public houses in Southwell. To have a drink in each hostelry in the same evening takes stamina and a strong head. But soon the challenge will not be quite so great. The Portland Arms in King Street is to close thereby reducing the number to a mere dozen. The owners, Whitbreads, have decided to sell and not continue as licensed premises. To date landlord, John Crepeau, does not know where he will go. But he definitely wants to stay in the trade. John Crepeau is a French Canadian. In his childhood he recalls taking food to the lumberjacks in the forest in a horse and sleigh. The family moved to the United States where John started work with a firm of water well drillers. In 1928 he moved to France...he met the girl who was to be his wife. They had two daughters but in 1937 she was killed in a road accident...With the outbreak of the Second World War John served with the Royal Army Service Corps attached to the Free French Forces as an interpreter. He was transferred to the Free French Air Force. At the end of the war John decided to move to Canada...after his return to England he moved to the Portland...With the departure of John Crepeau Southwell will be losing one of its most colourful landlords and the marathon drinkers will lose one of their ports of call.

Brewery links. The *Portland Arms* had for many years brewed its own beer but, like many other town public houses by the end of the nineteenth century, it was more economic to be a tied house. Consequently, by 1895 William Allen's, Worksop and Retford Brewery, had taken over the pub. In 1969 they too were bought out by the Whitbread Brewery and almost immediately Whitbread decided to sell the *Portland Arms,* but not as a public house. Ever since then there has been a small shopping arcade, named after the old pub.

Red Lion

Situation. There is a real mystery as to where the *Red Lion* was situated since existing evidence gives no precise location. The fact that a number of the landlords came from the Woodward and Cox families suggest the inn was either in Westhorpe or Easthorpe. Could the *Red Lion* have been the former name of the *Lord Nelson* (later the *Dumbles*)? Both the *Red Lion* and the *Lord Nelson* had strong connections with the Woodward family, but against this argument there is evidence that the inn still existed in 1815; additionally the *Lord Nelson* was described as an inn as early as 1814.

WEAVING.

THE CUSTOM-WEAVERS in *Southwell,* and the adjacent villages, finding themselves under the necessity of raising their Wages, on account of the advanced price of all kinds of necessaries of life, have this day met at the Red Lion, in *Southwell* aforesaid; and request leave to inform their customers, that they have agreed and concluded to lay one additional Halfpenny per Yard Weaving, upon plain Linens, Woolseys, &c. &c. also One Penny per Yard upon Ticking, common Table Linen, Woollens, &c. and in proportion for figured work; charging for the overshot cloth.

*** This alteration to commence on New-year's-day next.

Southwell. Nov. 24, 1792.

A notice from a local paper in 1792 which indicates the Custom Weavers held an urgent meeting at the **Red Lion***. (NJ December 8 1792).*

There are several advertisements in the *Nottingham Journal* from 1760 to 1815 regarding sales and meetings at the *Red Lion*, but nothing beyond that. There is no reference to the inn in *Pigot's 1819 Trade Directory* and we must wonder whether it changed its name or, as with one or two other inns in the town, was demolished to provide wider roads for the increasing number of coaching and carrying vehicles.

Activities. Like many public houses at this time, the *Red Lion* carried out regular sales on its premises from 1770-1810. The *Nottingham Journal* on March 10th 1810 reported that there was to be a sale '*At the house of Mrs.Woodward, the Sign of the Red Lion in Southwell on March 26th. A leasehold estate called Sacrista. Further particulars – Mr G Hodgkinson'*.

As with several of the larger inns, the *Red Lion* had rooms that could be used for meetings of local groups and also for administrative dealings. Two pieces of evidence support this. Firstly in 1792 a newspaper advertisement shows the inn was used by the Custom Weavers. Secondly, the *Red Lion* was also in use twenty years earlier for the bankruptcy hearing of a Westhorpe tanner.

We know very little of the innkeepers except that Henry Woodward and his wife were licensees. In the final evidence that we have in 1815, a Mrs.Cox was said to be the licensee.[29]

Name. The significance of the *Red Lion* as a choice of name, springs from the fact that lions have always been great signboard favourites. There are over 900 *Red Lion* signs in England, second only to the Crown in popularity. The *Red Lion* is probably not derived from the national coat of arms but more likely from the badge of Edward III.

Shoulder of Mutton

Location. The *Shoulder of Mutton*, a private residence since its closure in 1974, was situated at 46 Westgate, close to the junction with Nottingham Road and not far from the old cinema on the other side of the road. For many years it was affectionately known as the *Shoulder*.

NJ February 10th 1810 **To Be Sold by Auction**
A good accustomed public house known by the Sign of the Shoulder of Mutton, with complete Offices, Stable and Yardroom; also eight tenements and Dwellinghouses adjoining or near thereto occupied by J.Smalley, W.Norman, J.Terry, R.Wootton, S.Kerry E.Elkington, -Slater and J.Hall

Early history. Evidence shows it was a public house in the 1790s and possibly even earlier. In those early years when there was a marked absence of specialised public buildings in the town, the *Shoulder* acted as a centre for sales of property and also as a place where legal and financial business could be conducted. One example of this was reported in the *Nottingham Weekly Express* 1887 when an inquest was held there.[30] Its major role, however, was to serve the local Westgate community, particularly in relation to sporting activities. There was a brick building at the bottom of the rear garden that was used as a changing room by football clubs and the public house was also used by running clubs. As may be seen today, the building is quite substantial. A newspaper advertisement in 1810 indicates that there was considerable property to the rear, including offices, stable and yardroom.

*Dorothy Towers, the last victualler, standing in front of the **Shoulder of Mutton** shortly before its closure in 1975. (Roland Towers)*

Description. According to Roland Towers, the son of the last landlord, the Tap room was on the left of the central passage and contained seats, in the style of church pews, all round the walls with an amazing old table, which might well have been a butcher's slab, in the centre and the bar at the back. Behind the bar was the Snug (smoke room) which could only hold about 10 or 15 people and which was also furnished with pew seats. To the right of the passage was the Games Room, a long room with an open fireplace on the right and a marvellous old oak cupboard in the left corner. This room, which also had a piano, was the ideal size for playing darts, dominoes and table skittles. Upstairs there were bedrooms which in the nineteenth century were used by lodgers, travellers and, tradition has it, by billeted soldiers during the Napoleonic Wars and later during the First World War. Outside at the back there was a skittles alley and further back at the top of the garden were piggeries and a small brick building, the 'Gang Hut', which was used for many years by football teams for changing and later by local youths, according to Roland Towers, for chatting up girls and for having a secret smoke. Outside, at the front and to the right, there is still a small brick building which was known, when Roland Towers was living there, as the 'bottle house'; formerly it could well have been used by a butcher as a slaughterhouse, since there were still many meat hooks hanging on the beams.

Wartime and post-war memories. There are still people who can recall being served beer from a large jug, brought from the cellar, clearly before the time when pumps were installed. Many people still remember the *Shoulder* for its outdoor skittles alley. Charlie Grant has vivid memories of accompanying his uncle to the *Shoulder* and seeing him win a pig following a skittle competition. His uncle took the pig immediately down to Steel's, the butcher, to be slaughtered and it was promptly on the table for Saturday tea! Several people I spoke to had vivid memories of the strong link between the *Shoulder* and the Dance Hall at the Ideal Cinema, nearly opposite the old inn. The weekend dances were not only popular with local Southwellians but also with many youths, especially miners, from neighbouring towns and villages, who would come in by bus and get off next to the *Shoulder*. Roland Towers recalls how his father would instruct his staff to have three pints of beer ready on the bar for each miner when they ran in from the bus. Suitably fortified, the youths would then move over the road and dance to the music of 'Bert Brown and the OK Revellers', more widely known as 'Bert Brown and the Bucket Bashers'!

If they 'pulled' a girl they would usually go straight back to the *Shoulder* and order another three pints for themselves and brandy and Babycham for the girls. Fighting after the dances had finished was not uncommon and many a time Roland Towers' father had to wipe blood off the pavement in front of the pub. 'Jock' Grant recalls that in these 'emergency' situations the landlord, Geoff Boonham, would regularly request 'Jock's' assistance. They had served in the army together during the Second World War. Two other customs that were common practice were that local women would often queue up in the central passage for a jug of mild to take back home and that farmers and farm labourers would prefer to stand in the central passage and drink rather than going into any of the rooms.

Pub characters. All public houses have their regular 'characters' and the *Shoulder* was no exception. The fifties and sixties was the age of the 'Teddy Boy' and the *Shoulder* had their share. One particular Teddy Boy was Tommy Hayward, who grew his hair very long and stylish until the first day he entered the army and met up with the Sergeant Major. Another 'character' was 'Clemmie' Postle, who came into the pub every Sunday lunchtime, bringing with him six eggs. He would promptly drink six pints of Guinness and drop an egg into each – then go home for his dinner! Several people well remember Cecil Marrison, who bred goats off Halloughton Road. Wearing his working 'goats' clothing he would wander into the Tap Room, pipe blazing with Redbreast tobacco, and create quite a stir from the strong smell on his clothes! Charlie Watts did a regular delivery round to the *Shoulder* and he is well remembered by many late to middle aged men for 'doing his bit' for sex education in the town by making condoms available at the back of the inn for a reasonable price.

A group of regular clients in the Tap Room at the **Shoulder of Mutton** *in the late 1960s. From left to right Margaret Pitchford, not known, George Pitchford, Jack Beckett, Ernie?, Geoff Swift and Ken Butler. (Roland Towers)*

Landlords. The landlords at the *Shoulder of Mutton* tended to be very long serving. John Smith (c1810-1840) and Job Richardson (c1865-1890) were two good examples. In the Victorian age it was quite usual for publicans to have other occupations in order to boost the family income and John Slater at the *Shoulder* was a case in point. He was also a bricklayer and postmaster. In the twentieth century Fred Scarborough was another long serving landlord, being in post from 1890-1920. It was rather fitting that the last landlords, before closure in 1975, Roland and Dorothy Towers also served twenty years.

Closure. The *Shoulder* had been a tied house with Warwick and Richardson since the end of the nineteenth century. By 1975 first John Smith's Brewery then finally Courage had ownership. It was Courage who, in 1975, decided to close the *Shoulder* along with the *Grapes*, further along the road. It is clear to Roland Towers that the closure of the Ideal Cinema and Dance Hall in the early 1960s was a major factor – there was a marked loss of trade. This decline led to his mother closing the Games Room, except for use by private parties. Two other contributory factors to the closure were competition from the *Reindeer*, which had recently been refurbished, and the *Shoulder's* location, sited a fair distance from the town centre.

Southwell Brewery

For a short period in the late nineteenth century there appeared to be two breweries in the town. As well as the Westgate Brewery trade directories and brewery records inform us that there was also Southwell Brewery. *Kelly's 1881 Directory* and the *Century of British Brewers 1890-2004* both refer to Southwell Brewery in King Street with George Langtry as manager in 1881-2. Around this time the brewery seems to have been taken over by the firm, Smith and Nephew, who themselves became part of the larger Worksop and Retford Brewery. It was likely Worksop and Retford would have kept the brewery open for another few years as they had three other 'tied' houses in the town as well as other houses in nearby villages. According to *Friedrich's Gazetteer of the British Isles* Southwell Brewery was still in existence in 1906 under the ownership of Smith and Nephew though by this time it is likely that, as with the Westgate Brewery, the building would have been used as a depot and distribution centre. There are no brewers in the town mentioned in the trade directories after 1900.

Where would Southwell Brewery have been located? The brewery would very likely have been close to or at the *Admiral Rodney* in King Street. In the 1869 *Morris Directory* the publican there, John Dixon, was described as a brewer and maltster. Ten years later in *Wright's Directory* of 1869 his wife, Elizabeth Dixon, was mentioned as one of the two brewers in the town. We also know from Newark and Southwell licensing records that the *Rodney* had become tied to the Worksop and Retford Brewery, which had acquired the Smith and Nephew Brewery in 1881.

Westgate Beerhouse

Whilst we have evidence that there was a beerhouse in Westgate from 1835 to around 1870 we have no exact location for this building. Some beerhouses were given titles, others were simply named after the street. This one seems to fit into the latter category. Most opened shortly after the Beerhouse Act of 1830 and many had closed by 1870 owing to pressure placed on the government from the Temperance Movement to control the spread of public houses, especially beerhouses. In the case of the Westgate Beerhouse trade directories tell us it was still open in 1864 but that is the final entry.

Beerhouse Keepers. We do have information that the beerhouse keeper in 1835 was William Parker, who had a second occupation as a bricklayer. In 1864 we find the keeper is Thomas Leek, who was also a plumber and glazier.

*An advertisement for **Westgate Brewery** in 1900 shortly before it was taken over by Marstons. Herbert F. Ealand was connected with the brewery for many years and served in a number of capacities. (Mary West)*

Westgate Brewery

Situation. *Westgate Brewery*, sometimes referred to as *Ealand's Brewery*, was situated on the south side of Westgate, close to the junction with Nottingham Road. It opened in the 1860s and was demolished in 1931, replaced, on virtually the same footprint, by the Ideal Cinema. Why was that site chosen for a brewery? It is likely that earlier, on the same site, there had been a maltings with kiln and offices. Not only do trade directories indicate this, but when in 1903 Westgate Brewery was up for sale the maltings also was included.[31] In recent years the old cinema has been redeveloped into an award winning block of apartments.

Early history. The *Breweries of the British Isles* reveals that the brewery opened in 1876-77 with William Taylor of Stanton-on-Wolds as brewer. Compared with the nearby Newark breweries it would have been relatively small. How many public houses would it have provided with beer? The only evidence we have on this matter is that in 1903-4 when it was sold to *Marston, Thompson and Son Ltd.*, the brewery was sold along with ten public houses for £3,000. By 1884 Sprigg and Henry had taken over with Charles Francis Henry as brewer. Brewery records then show that three years later C.F Henry was declared bankrupt, with the Goodwin Brothers in Newark handling the sale.[32] It appears that the brewery passed into the hands of Herbert Fawsit Ealand, who became identified with the brewery for many years, even after it had been taken over in 1903.

Westgate Brewery in the early years of the twentieth century, showing the brewery was then under the ownwership of Marston, Thompson and Evershed from Burton on Trent. They purchased the brewery in 1903 and sold it in 1931. (Dean and Chapter of Southwell Minster.)

Small breweries had difficulty then as now competing with the larger brewery companies, and in 1904 Ealand's *Westgate Brewery* was purchased by *J.Marston, Thompson and Son Ltd* of Burton on Trent. The following year, Evershed amalgamated with J.Marston, Thompson and Co. to make *Marston, Thompson and Evershed.* Eric Fower, the Marston's historian is certain that in 1904-5 Marstons would not have used the building for brewing as it would not have been economically viable. It would have been used as a depot and distribution centre for Marston's ten local public houses. An agent or manager would have been appointed to arrange deliveries and inspections at the ten public houses. In addition an off licence would have been obtained to sell beer, wine and spirits at the old brewery. This view is supported by the fact that many local people have still in their possession bottles from Ealand's Brewery dating from the early 1900s. The *Newark and Southwell Licensing records* also support this view and record that Herbert Ealand continued to work at the *Westgate Brewery* as manager and licensee along with agent Frank Ewers, who remained until the brewery's demolition in 1931.

Closure. Quite simply, the year 1931 was in the worst period of the 'Great Depression' when many thousands of people were unemployed and the resulting lack of trade affected brewery companies and public houses just like most other businesses. With the level of unemployment being very high, clearly there was less demand for beer, wine and spirits. The licensing entry states coldly, *13th February 1931 'No renewal application on account of premises being demolished'*. The site was soon occupied when the Ideal Cinema was built virtually on the same footprint.

Westhorpe Beerhouse

Situation. This beerhouse was situated close to the junction of roads in Westhorpe, opposite the *Grapes* and close to the *Dumbles* (then the *Lord Nelson*). There was no lack of 'watering holes' in Westhorpe at this time! Many beerhouses, resulting from the 1830 Beerhouse Act, lasted a comparatively short time and by 1860 had closed. The *Westhorpe Beerhouse* seems to have survived longer than most in spite of the fact there were a number of public houses in this community. Clearly the Westhorpe agricultural labourers and framework knitters were a thirsty lot!

Beerhouse keepers. *Westhorpe Beerhouse* was very much linked with the local Fairholm family, who were also wheelwrights. William and Mary Fairholm are named alternately as beerhouse keeper in trade directories over the period 1830-60. The Fairholm family were succeeded in 1864 by John Clarke and by James Everington in 1872.

White Swan

Situation. The *White Swan*, for years also known as the *Cock House*, was situated at the top end of King Street, opposite Burgage House. Following its closure in 1921, this substantial three storey building was converted into shops at the front and private apartments at the back. At present the Minster Garage occupies part of what was the front of the historic inn.

Early history. The present building dates from around 1800, though from RP Shilton's *History of Southwell* we learn that there had been an earlier inn on the premises. It would have been one of the town's largest inns. We have evidence from two plans a century ago that on the ground floor was a Tap Room, Smoke Room and Billiard Room.[33] Upstairs there was living accommodation for the landlord and additional bedroom space for travellers. At the rear of the property was a large yard with a skittle alley, stabling for eight horses, a Brewhouse, Barn and Piggeries for twenty pigs. There was also a number of cottages adjoining and belonging to the *White Swan*.

The landlord, William Gibson, and his wife with their baby outside the **White Swan** *c*1900. Mr.Gibson also worked as a farmer at Normanton. (Philip Robinson.)

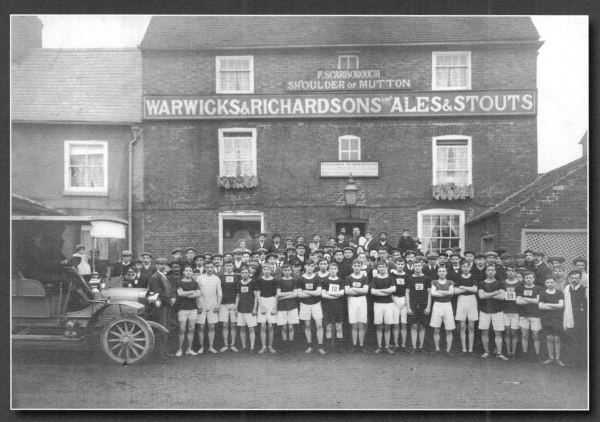

*A Marathon Race from the **Shoulder of Mutton** to Sutton-in-Ashfield (Dec.19 1908). The landlord, Fred Scarborough, can be seen standing to the right of the doorway. (Roland Towers).*

*A Hedgehog Race taking place outside the **Hearty Goodfellow** in the 1940s.
The central character is 'Squint' Stephenson, who is surrounded by his large family.
Left to right – Mary Stephenson, Edwin?, Alice Wood, Jonny, Brenda and Alice Stephenson, William (Squint)
Stephenson, ? Burton, Mr Burton, Muriel Chamberline, ? Burton, Annie Postle. (Brian and Rebecca Jollands)*

ARTHUR GUINNESS SON & CO. (PARK ROYAL) LTD.

VISIT TO PARK ROYAL BREWERY

SOUTHWELL & DISTRICT
LICENSED VICTUALLERS' ASSOCIATION

JULY 23rd 1957

Southwell and District Licensed Victuallers 1957. (Roland Towers).

Southwell Licensed Victuallers, fifty years later, December 2007. (Mollie Toy).
Left to right - (back) Dave Iremonger (insert) Neil McKechen, Nick Turner, Brian Jollands,
Larry Dukes, Insp.Andy Gan (front) Amanda Pearce (insert) Chris Davis, Helen Hardy,
Claire Johnson-Cooper, Becky Jollands, Paul Inman, John Pearce (insert)

Wall Paintings at the *Saracen's Head*
There are rooms on both floors where there are walls richly decorated with wall paintings.
Some of these have been identified as Elizabethan.

Bramley Room, to the right of the hotel entrance

King Charles suite, a close up

Inn Signs

In 1393 King Richard II compelled landlords to erect signs outside their premises.
The legislation stated *Whosoever shall brew ale in the town with the intention of selling it must hang out a sign, otherwise he shall forfeit his ale.* This law was passed in order to make alehouses easily visible to passing ale inspectors. Another important factor, was that during the Middle Ages many people would have been illiterate and so pictures were more useful than words for identifying an alehouse.

Inn sign at the **Crown**
Many inn signs have royal and aristocratic associations as a mark of showing allegiance to the monarchy.

Inn sign at the **Wheatsheaf**
Much work in the eighteenth century would have centred on agriculture and many inn signs have traditionally been pictures of tools or products linked with agriculture.

Inn sign at the **Saracen's Head**
In the twelfth and thirteenth centuries noble families, whose members had taken part in the Crusades, often included a Saracen's Head as part of their coat of arms.
It was then passed on to inn signs.

Inn sign at the **Reindeer**
Animals have traditionally been a popular feature for inn signs, many animals featuring as part of aristocratic coats of arms.

Activities. Evidence suggests that the *White Swan* was one of the liveliest of the town's inns, particularly in the early 1800s when there were plenty of commercial and recreational activities on the nearby Burgage. The inn and its landlord, John Elsam, made a good living from the horse races and cattle fairs which took place on the Burgage at Whitsun and at other times of the year. But it was as a place to view cock-fighting that the *White Swan* had established its reputation. In his *History of Southwell* (1818) RP Shilton refers to *'the house of Mr John Elsam, now the White Swan, largely rebuilt, but which was called for ages by the name of the Cockhouse.'* As far back as 1697 from the Chancery Court records we learn that, *'It is said in Southwell that George Cartwright seldom goes to bed more than twice a week sober and that he has been connected with a woman living at a public house at the sign of 'The Cock'.*[34]

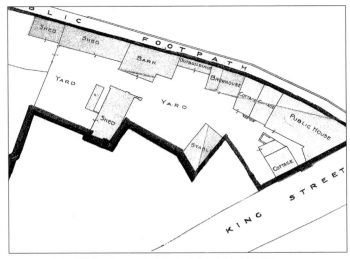

A plan of the **White Swan** in 1907. (NA DD/M 71/247)

As well as its association with cockfighting, the *White Swan*, according to John Holmes in the early 1800s, was notorious for providing other even less savoury services. In his memoirs, John Holmes states *'Some young ladies from Newark took a house of Mr Elsam by the White Swan. It was soon found that the house was kept as a house of ill fame and it was ever after called Spiby Hall'*. Nevertheless there was a more 'respectable' side to the *White Swan*. The Elsam family, as landlords, were asked to hold many sales on their premises as the following newspaper extract indicates.

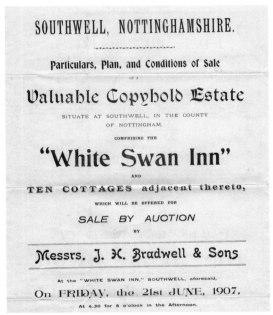

NJ- June 6 1806 – To Be Sold By Auction
Lot 1 ALL that Upton Field Close, now or late in the occupation of Mr. Thomas Bagnell, containing 3 Acres, 2 Roods, Tythe free.
Lot 5 Also a Piece of land in Buckhill, containing 1 Rood, 23 Perches.
Lot 6 Also that Piece of land in Southwell Meadow, adjoining the Cotton-Mill, containing 2 Acres, 2 Roods, 2 Perches.
..Further particulars ..at Mr John Elsam's White Swan.

Another sign of its popularity amongst the working classes was the fact that the landlords of the *White Swan* provided pub checks, or tokens, as an alternative to the regular payment of cash. The pub tokens could have been used by individuals or by local friendly societies.

The sale of the **White Swan** in 1907, near its closure date. (NA DD/M 71/247)

Landlords. The Elsam family was a major influence in the first part of the nineteenth century. John and Sarah Elsam ran the house together from c1790-1830. John's son, Thomas Elsam, had two additional occupations, both linked with his job as a publican. He was shown in the trade directories as being a maltster and hop grower.[35] Other publicans with multiple occupations were Matthew Revill who, in the 1869 directory, was reported to be a blacksmith and William Gibson, who was a farmer in 1900. Records show that the *White Swan* had its own brewhouse and it is likely that beer was brewed here until the late 1800s. By 1900 the public house was tied to William Allen's, Worksop and Retford Brewery and this remained the case until the public house closed in 1921.

*Pub checks, or tokens, were regularly used by landlords at the **White Swan** as an alternative to cash for the benefit of working men who were on a low income. Note the landlord's initials, SS, (Sam Stokes) in the centre. (Grenville Chamberlain)*

Closure. By 1900 local magistrates were increasingly concerned that there were too many public houses in Southwell and particularly in King Street. It is mainly for this reason that they refused to renew the licence of the *Black Bull* in 1908.[36]

William IV

Maythorne Cottages today on Lower Kirklington Road

Situation. This beerhouse was located on the corner of Maythorne Lane and Lower Kirklington Road, nearly opposite the northern entrance to Norwood Park. There were a number of cottages on this site and tradition has it that the *William IV* occupied the most western of the cottages. The cottages are still there today though converted into one property.

Historical background. There are more public houses named after William IV than any other monarch. William succeeded to the throne in 1830, the same year that the Beer Act was passed by Parliament, actively promoting the establishment of beerhouses as a means of discouraging the consumption of gin. Trade directories inform us that the *William IV* was a beerhouse and was open for business in the second half of the nineteenth century. George Gleadle was manager and the beerhouse was also known as the *Garden Gate*.[36] Its clientele would have been residents of Maythorne, workers at the Maythorne Silk Mill and agricultural labourers from Norwood Park.

Closure. We have no precise evidence as to when the *William IV* closed but it is likely that it must have been around 1900. In a letter to Professor Barley of Nottingham University in 1977, Mrs.K Coulthard, a former resident of Maythorne Cottages, wrote, *'the story is that the owners of the Silk Mill down the lane, Beans and Johnson's of Halam and Sir William Starkey's grandfather bought the property and closed the inn because their staff gathered there instead of working'*.[37] In support of this explanation Sir John Starkey told me recently that he remembers that his grandfather's butler lived at Maythorne Cottages well into the twentieth century.

Woolpack

Situation. We know that the *Woolpack* was situated in Westgate, but we have no precise knowledge as to where in Westgate. It has been suggested that the inn could have been formerly known as the *Shoulder of Mutton* but evidence from the *Nottingham Journal* seems to contradict this. We have clear evidence from a sale notice that the *Shoulder of Mutton* existed in 1800 and fourteen years later in 1814 that public house was up for auction. The *Woolpack*, however, regularly featured in newspapers during the same period, 1790-1814. Could the *Woolpack* have been a former name of the *Lord Nelson*, now the *Dumbles*? Whilst the dates fit, written pieces of evidence refer to the *Woolpack* being *'centrally situate'* in the town; the *Lord Nelson* was in Westhorpe, which is clearly not.

Another interesting and more likely possibility is that today's 52 Westgate (see photograph) was originally the *Woolpack*. Molly Broadberry recalls that when she lived there in the 1950s, her parents used to say that they had been told that the house had originally been an old coaching inn. Certainly the present house, yard, outbuildings and garden have similar features to the descriptions in the sale notices in the early 1800s, as shown below. The main part of the house dates from the late eighteenth century and at the back of the property there is an ample garden with fruit trees and yard with a number of outbuildings, including an old stable.

*52 Westgate – a possible location for the **Woolpack** (Terry Pearce)*

Description. The information we have on the *Woolpack* covers the years 1793-1814. I have found no further references in either trade directories or census returns. But we do have contemporary descriptions of the property. Three sales of the *Woolpack* in 1793, 1811 and 1814 reveal that the house contained *'excellent Cellaring, large Yard, Stable, good Garden'*. The 1811 and 1814 newspaper notices also speak of two or three tenements in the yard. These tenements, we are told, were occupied by John Leeson in 1811 and by John Platt and Arthur Easle in 1814. The earlier notice from the *Nottingham Journal* on the 5th January 1793, reports that the sale will also include *'eight dwelling houses and a very good garden, planted with fruit trees and a good shop.'*

With regard to activities at the public house, again we know little, except that sales of other properties were carried out on the premises. The ownership of the *Woolpack* was in the hands of Mr. Holles in 1811 and a Mr. Jackson in 1814.

Name. The name, *Woolpack*, for a public house inn sign comes as no surprise in the eighteenth century, as England was mainly a rural country, relying on the land to provide basic food supplies. Animals were an important part of the agricultural scene, with sheep being reared for their wool as well as their meat.

> AT SOUTHWELL, NOTTINGHAMSHIRE.
>
> ——
>
> DESIRABLE SITUATION.
>
> TO BE SOLD BY PUBLIC AUCTION,
>
> By Mr. ROBINSON,
>
> *(With immediate Possession, if required)*
>
> Upon the Premises, on Saturday the 2d Day of July, 1814, at Five o'Clock in the Afternoon, (subject to such Conditions of Sale as will be then produced) in One Lot,
>
> ALL that well-built and good-accustomed PUBLIC HOUSE, with convenient sized Chambers, excellent Cellaring, large Yard, Stable, good Garden, and other Conveniencies to the same belonging, centrically situate in the Town of Southwell aforesaid, known by the Sign of the " Woolpack," in the Occupation of Mr. Jackson, the Owner.
>
> Also, TWO TENEMENTS in the said Yard, in good Repair, in the several Occupations of John Platts, and Arthur Easle.
>
> * * Further Particulars may be known of the said Mr. JACKSON; or at the Office of the Auctioneer, in Mansfield.

*Sale of the **Woolpack**, 1814. (NJ June 25 1814)*

Workman's Rest

Situation. The *Workman's Rest,* now once more a private residence, was situated at the western end of a row of houses just past and to the south of Sunnyside Cottages. Today there is a heritage plaque on the wall outside explaining the significance of the *Rest* to the community of Westhorpe. Back in the eighteenth century the house belonged to a wealthy man, known locally as the 'Squire', whose labourers occupied the cottages alongside. The nearby arch was the entrance to a courtyard for horse drawn vehicles. In 1839 the house was sold by auction at the *Saracen's Head Inn*.

Early history. It was bought by the mother of General Warrand, the owner of Westhorpe Hall in the early Victorian period. Mrs Warrand was concerned for the welfare of the local tenants and labourers and so set out to convert the residence into a Working Man's Club or Institute. According to Marjorie Hustwayte and Penny Young's *Holy Trinity Church, Southwell (1846-96)* Mrs.Warrand had long recognised that *'the surest way to promote Temperance was to provide a counter-attraction to the public house and the Workman's Rest and the Mission Room - placed most generously at the service of the Vicar of Holy Trinity - were her institutions. Trustees included the Vicar, the Rev. HK Warrand, Mr. JM Wand and Sir William Hicking of Brackenhurst Hall.'*

At Mrs. SMITH'S, the SARACEN'S HEAD INN, SOUTHWELL

At Four o'clock in the Afternoon, in one or more Lots and subject to such Conditions as will be then produced;

ALL THAT CAPITAL

MESSUAGE

Situate at Westhorpe, Southwell, in the occupation of Mrs. Birkett, comprising Two Sitting Rooms, Kitchen Back Kitchen, and Pantries, on the ground Floor; Four Bed Rooms in the Chamber Story; and Three spacious Attics, Arched Cellars, and detached Wash House, Bake House, and Dairy.

The Out-Buildings consist of an excellent Stable for Eight Horses, with Two Granaries over it, large Barn, Cow House, a Fold Yard, walled round, convenient Piggery, &c.; There are also on the Premises, and at a short distance from the House a large Barn, and several extensive Drying and Cart Sheds, and other Buildings, Vats, &c., which have lately been used in carrying on the business of a Tanner, for which purpose the Premises are very desirable.

The above Buildings stand on a Site containing about 1A. 2R. 0P. of Land, part of which is conveniently laid out in Gardens and Orchards, forming together a desirable Investment

ALSO, THE FOLLOWING CLOSES OF VALUABLE MEADOW AND PASTURE LAND, VIZ.:

	A.	R.	P.		A.	R.	P.
The Long Hollows, containing by Estimation	3	0	0	AND,			
The Ridge Gate or West Field Close	2	0	12	One Land in Southwell open field, containing by Estimation	0	3	0
The Cold Hill Close	1	2	36	One Land in Bath Field	0	2	0
The Stubbings Field Close	4	0	0	One Land in Halloughton Dale Field	0	3	0

AND ALSO,

All that POST WIND MILL, standing near the Road leading from Southwell to Halloughton, working one Pair of French and one Pair of Grey Stones, with the Dressing Machine, two Sets of Cylinders, and other Machinery; together with all those two undivided third parts or shares (the whole into three equal parts or shares being considered as divided,) of and in the Land on which the Mill stands, containing about one Rood.

The above Estate is Copyhold, of the Manor of Southwell, (Fine small and certain) excepting a small part of the Homestead which is Freehold.

For further particulars or a View of the Estate apply to Mr. BRIGGS, on the Premises, or to Mr. NICHOLSON, Architect, or to

MESSRS. BARROW & FALKNER, SOLICITORS, SOUTHWELL.

SOUTHWELL, NOVEMBER, 21, 1839.

C. & W. RIDGE, PRINTERS, MARKET-PLACE.

*A poster from 1839 showing the sale of the Westhorpe house which was soon to become the **Workman's Rest**. (NA DD/M 105/32)*

Activities. According to a number of local 'Westhorpers', including Dorothy Hugill, there was a large room upstairs, the Meeting or Parish Room, which in later years came to be used by local ladies, led by the wife of the Vicar of Holy Trinity, Westhorpe's church. This was also the place where the local men and the youth of Westhorpe would meet and play billiards and skittles. Dorothy Hugill recalls that access to this upper room was by an external staircase, which still exists to the left of the arch. In another upper room over the archway, church services were held, in what was called the Mission Room. Outside there was a sizeable courtyard with a number of outbuildings, including stables for eight horses. One of the ground floor rooms to the right of the arch, now 31 Westhorpe, was used as a Sub Post Office. For many years there was a letter box in the wall of No 35.

The *Workman's Rest* supplied a real need in the life of the parish. Apart from its popularity with workmen, who regularly made use of the recreational facilities, it was also the focus for much of the church's social life - Mothers' Meetings, Bible Classes, Girls' Friendly Society parties and concerts. Whilst the foundation of the *Rest* was clearly linked with the promotion of temperance, there are local people still alive who recall that by the 1930s there had been a relaxation of the 'soft drinks only' ruling, and for certain functions the *Rest* obtained beer from the *Grapes*, across the road.

Over the years many local people got much pleasure from the two billiard tables. Geoff Dodsworth remembers back in the late 1930s, when he lived on Westgate, that he learnt to play billiards at the *Rest*. Geoff recalls that it was a big room and, although there was a coal fire, it was rather cold but you couldn't just muscle your way towards the warmth as there was an accepted 'pecking' order as to who could sit close to the fire. Other recreational activities available were table tennis, skittles, dominoes, cards, whist drives and bagatelle as well as newspapers and refreshments. In their booklet, Marjorie Hustwayte and Penny Young stress that the *'Rest also sought to provide education through its Night School lectures, its Reading Room and Library* (with writing tables), *whose maximum annual circulation of books reached over 7,000'.*

Other activities at the *Rest* centred on the Westhorpe ladies, organised by Mrs Coghill, wife of the vicar of Holy Trinity. A Sewing Circle made garments for the children of needy families in the area. As the Holy Trinity booklet reports, *'The Sewing Circle's fame spread with the inclusion of the recipe for "Southwell Sewing Meeting Tea Cake" in the Newark Cookery Book'.* Another extremely useful resource at the *Rest* was the Warwick Penny Bank. The Holy Trinity booklet comments that *'deposits were made throughout the year, pay-out day being a great event when pieces of Christmas cake were distributed to the depositors, who occasionally numbered well over 800. The amount paid out could be as much as £2,646. 12s. 5d (in 1920)'.*

The following extract from a report on the condition of agricultural labourers in the district gives a good idea of how the *Rest* was used at the turn of the century.

*A drawing by Christine Measures of the **Workman's Rest**.*

In the twentieth century the *Rest* was used by Westhorpe Cricket Club, who played at Westhorpe's Top Ground. The club's inaugural meeting was held in April 1930. Between the wars the *Rest* committee felt a rent of £12 should be charged so Whist Drives were introduced to help raise the money. During the two World Wars the *Rest* was available to soldiers billeted and training in the area. They were especially keen on using the billiard tables. From 1939-45 Mrs.Mosedale served coffee to the troops stationed at the private houses in Westhorpe. In November 1939 the *Rest* celebrated its Jubilee as the following newspaper extract shows.

*Newark Advertiser – Nov.1 1939 **Jubilee Year for Workman's Rest***
The Workman's Rest has just entered on its 50th season and in wartime the committee hope
it will be able to provide a social club for Westhorpe. The club is run by a committee from
Holy Trinity and the amenities include billiards, table tennis, skittles and card games.
The committee hope to have a social and whist drives during the winter months.
They will be arranged to make full use of the moon so that people will not be prevented
from attending by the blackout's causing walking difficulties.

Managers. As the *Rest* was a workers' institute and not a public house it had a manager, rather than a landlord. Three families played an important part in filling that role. Thomas and Anne Daybell managed the *Rest* from c1860-95. Thomas Daybell was also stated in the censuses to be a coachman and grocer.[38] The Sensecall family took over the *Rest,* including the Sub Post Office, in the early 1900s, to be followed by Wilfred Lancelot Kendall and his wife from 1923-46. Geoff Dodsworth remembers 'Wilf' Kendall living on the premises.

Closure. The increased rent became a financial burden and the new vicar, the Rev.Garry Stephens, in the late 1940s decided to give up the house as a workmen's institution, so the billiard tables and possessions were sold. Trinity Church for a time still kept one room as a Church Meeting room, but in 1951 Group Captain Hanmer, the landlord, sold the property to Eric Martin, who later sold it to Douglas Gascoine. The cottages, including the *Workman's Rest,* were due to be demolished but a Conservation Group was formed and the demolition was fortunately prevented.

9. Surviving Inns and Public Houses

Admiral Rodney

Early history. This old inn is situated in the centre of King Street in the same location as an earlier inn. There is still some uncertainty regarding the inn's name before 1780 but we do know from George Hodgkinson's *Georgian Diary* that in 1781 Samuel Bettinson's house was referred to as the *Rodney's Head*. [39] Admiral Rodney had become a national hero the previous year when the British navy gained a famous victory over the Spanish squadron at the Battle of Cape Vincent.

Description. As you stand in King Street and look across at the *Rodney* there would have been a carriage way on the left hand side, where today there is the doorway to the public bar. This enabled a coach and horses to drive all the way round the building to the stables and back onto the main street. Inside, the *Rodney* retains an authentic feel from the timber framed interior of the public bar with its low, original beams. One of the beams is reputed to have come from a ship, the HMS Rodney, whilst another is said to have originated in the bellringing gallery at Southwell Minster. Downstairs, refurbishment during the 1980s unearthed a well, possibly used for brewing the inn's own ale.

At the back of the inn is a function room, now used for commercial purposes, parties, tea dances and by many local organisations for their meetings. On the first floor there used to be a number of bedrooms providing accommodation for travellers, and a very large ballroom. Even though it desperately needs restoration, the old ballroom still has an air of grandeur with its impressive windows and musicians' balcony. In the 1940s the ballroom was used as a school run by the daughter of the landlord, Miss Thomas, a trained dancer. The school was later moved to Kirklington, where it became known as the 'Rodney School'. During the First World War the ballroom was converted into a casualty ward for returning wounded soldiers. In what is now a bar and outside seating area on the south side of the building there was formerly a livery stable, followed by an early motor garage.

*A coaching scene outside the **Admiral Rodney** just after the turn of the century. Albert Merryfield was innkeeper from 1907-15 and he was also proprietor at the **Saracen's Head.** Note also the inn was tied to Worksop and Retford Brewery. (Nottinghamshire County Council- Southwell Library)*

*The carriageway to the left hand side of the **Rodney**, as you stand in King Street. This photograph was taken in the early 1900s. The carriageway has now been integrated into the inn. (Nottinghamshire County Council –Southwell Library.)*

Commercial activities. At the height of the coaching age the inn and its yard would have been a hive of activity. Suprisingly perhaps, Southwell was well served by the coaching companies in the first half of the nineteenth century and the *Rodney*, like the *Saracen's Head*, the *Crown*, and to a lesser extent the *Reindeer,* would have been essential ports of call for a change of horses. In the 1820s the 'Negotiator' coach from Nottingham to Newark always stopped for a change of horses at the *Rodney* whilst the inn also served the 'Standard' coach travelling from Derby through to Newark.[40] Lastly, the inn had visits from the 'Royal Perseverance' *en route* from Nottingham to Gainsborough. Many of these coaches would have used the Leadenham- Southwell- Mansfield Turnpike, whose trustees held regular meetings at the *Rodney* over the years.

Apart from its major involvement in the town's coaching business, the *Rodney* was an important centre for all kinds of sales at a time when there was a marked absence of dedicated auction rooms and estate agencies. With its large function room the inn was an ideal venue for the sale of furniture, china, silver plate and books. It is interesting to note that to some extent the *Rodney* still fulfils this role today.

A further activity back in Georgian and Victorian Southwell was the use of the *Rodney* to conduct financial and legal business. In 1781 the local attorney, George Hodgkinson, regularly used the inn for such purposes, as on the 29th July when he *'delivered the lease to the hands of Samuel Bettinson (innkeeper)'*. With its status as a coaching inn, the *Rodney* would attract the custom of the local gentry and the business classes. This can be seen from references in local papers to dinners, dances, meetings and other celebrations that took place in the ballroom (or Assembly Room as it was also called). One such was the *Anniversary of Southwell Literary Society* which took place at the Archery ground but was followed by tea provided by the *Admiral Rodney*. Later, reported the *Newark Advertiser* on the 28th June 1855, there was dancing and other amusements.

Inter-war and post-war memories. Geoff Dodsworth recalls that in the 1940s the inn had its accommodation fully booked up for weeks with scientists from Canada and the United States who were involved in the exploration for oil at Eakring. He also remembers that in the 1930s the Scout group, which he belonged to, used the *Rodney* ballroom. In more recent years the function room, at the back of the *Rodney* has continued to host regular meetings (and celebrations) of local clubs and organisations. The British Legion at one time regularly met there. Three more recent examples of

*An auction of furniture at the **Rodney** in January 1867. Most large inns would have their own assembly room for social events and function room for commerce. (NA DD/M 71/235)*

these are the visits of Southwell and District Lions, Southwell Railway Club and Southwell Fishing Club. In line with its tradition of attracting people to dances in the ballroom, it is interesting to report that at the time of writing Salsa classes are being held weekly in the function room and there has also been a revival of Tea Dances.

The *Rodney* attracted its fair share of characters, including Billy Burrows. Herbert Lewin recalls patrolling down King Street as a Special Constable when he came across Billy's horse and dray parked outside the *Rodney* on the recently painted double yellow lines. *'Whose horse and dray is this?'* asked the Special Constable. *'My horse, constable'*, answered Billy. *'Mr Burrows, you're contravening the double yellow lines regulations'*, stated the Special Constable. *'Constable, I've worked my old mare hard all day. She was nodding off so I only came in for a drink to give her some rest'*. Billy got off!

Innkeepers. William Bettinson, innkeeper from c.1775 to 1820, was clearly a well known Southwell character. When he died in 1820 after forty-five years service he was given a special obituary in the *Nottingham Journal*. William Bettinson, like many other innkeepers, had another trade but it wasn't a trade connected with innkeeping. He was a hairdresser. George Hodgkinson writes in his diary, *'Paid Bettinson in full for a year's hairdressing.*[41] In his *History of Southwell* RP Shilton reveals that William Bettinson was an exceptionally patriotic and public spirited citizen. Not only did he subscribe in 1794 and 1798 to 'Loyal Aids' for raising local defence forces in case of a French invasion, but in 1804 he joined the *Loyal Southwell Volunteer Infantry*.

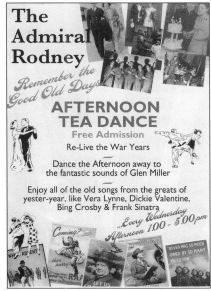

*A recent poster advertising 'Tea Dances', maintaining a long tradition of music and dance at the **Admiral Rodney**. (Neil McKendrick)*

*Mr.and Mrs.Merryfield, proprietors, unusually, of two inns, the **Admiral Rodney** and the **Saracen's Head**, in the early 1900s.*

William Bettinson was succeeded by his son, also William, and together they ended up serving the *Rodney* for sixty-five years. Fifteen years later the Dixon family took over the running of the old inn. In the trade directories between 1860 and 1880 both John and Elizabeth Dixon are described as 'brewers and maltsters'. Albert Merryfield (proprietor 1907-15) must have been a resourceful character for he was publican at the *Saracen's Head* at the same time. According to Kelly's *Directory* in 1912 Albert Merryfield had not only persuaded the RAC to select the *Rodney* as their headquarters but was also agent to the Midland Railway. The close link between the inn and the *Saracen's Head* was continued with the next proprietor, Frederick Heald serving both inns between the wars.

John and Wilfred Thomas kept the *Rodney* in the period after the Second World War. Geoff Dodsworth recalls the landlord always boasted at the bar that he could provide any drink that was requested. If he failed to do this he would give the customer free beer all night. Geoff and his friend always tried to find a variety of beer that the landlord would be unlikely to stock but never quite managed it though on one occasion, he recalls, they were one bottle away from achieving success.

One story that has echoes down the years concerns the *Rodney's* own resident friendly spirit, 'Ballroom Charlie'. During the First World War the *Rodney* ballroom was converted into a casualty hospital for wounded soldiers. One of these wounded soldiers, Charlie, sadly died at the *Rodney* but according to a number of sources his spirit still haunts the premises. Previous publicans, including Steve Church and Maurice Selby, noted in earlier years that visitors to the *Rodney* occasionally saw a face at the window of the ballroom door with the top of the soldier's uniform just visible. In addition to stories of 'sighting' a ghost, several people have commented on unexplained happenings in the *Rodney*. Margaret Church, wife of ex-landlord Dennis Church, remembers well one evening when a friend of her husband's, Jack, came to pick him up to go to a masonic meeting. Margaret Church offered Jack a chair in the big kitchen whilst he waited for her husband to get ready. When Dennis and Margaret returned to the kitchen they were taken aback by how ashen and shaken Jack had become. He muttered to them that some 'presence' had been tapping him on the shoulder. Margaret Church also told me of two other interesting occurences. Firstly their dog, a labrador, never wanted to go upstairs and secondly on more than one occasion cleaning ladies called for her to come because they felt a 'presence' was watching them. Margaret's son, Steve Church told me that when he lived for a time on his own in the top floor apartment he regularly heard unexplained footsteps on the next level. Alan Whalley, brother of ex-landlord Gordon, also informed me that when he stayed at the *Rodney* in the late 1960s he often felt a coldness, an eerie definite 'presence'. More recently, present landlord Neil McKechen, reported that one night he had left the *Rodney* having put out all the lights only to find the next morning that all the light bulbs at one side of the bar had been taken out and placed on the furniture by the side wall, close to the well.

Brewery links. There had been a brewhouse at the *Rodney* for many years but interestingly in the mid 1800s there are clear suggestions from the trade directories that the *Rodney*, or a small brewery near the *Rodney*, was supplying other local public houses with ale. In the *1869 Morris Directory,* publican, John Dixon, was described also as a brewer and malster. Ten years later, in *Wright's 1879 Directory*, his wife Elizabeth Dixon was mentioned as one of two brewers in the town. For further information on this matter please refer to page 28 *Southwell Brewery*. By the early 1900s the Worksop and Retford Brewery had ownership of the *Rodney* and trade directories and licensing records indicate the brewery used the *Rodney* as a depot and distribution centre. The *Newark Advertiser*, in 1903, has an interesting comment on the *Rodney's* link with the Worksop and Retford Brewery Company.

Newark Advertiser- February 25 1903

Much interest was occasioned on Thursday last on the arrival of the Worksop and Retford Brewery Company's motor, which brought over five tons of ale. The motor left Worksop for Southwell, a distance of 28 miles, at 7-00am and after delivering orders at Edingley and Halam reached the Southwell stores (Ad.Rodney) shortly after 12 noon, although so heavily laden. It had in addition a dray or trailer fixed behind, which was used for bottled goods and spirits. It was very easily manipulated and attracted much attention.

Bramley Apple

Description. The *Bramley Apple* is situated in Church Street, close to the Potwell Dyke. We have records that show there was an inn on this site as far back as the early 1780s. From that time to 1975, when it was temporarily closed, it was known as the *George and Dragon.* Following its reopening its name was changed to the *Bramley Apple,* after Southwell's famous apple, originating just down the road. We have very little evidence of how the building looked in the eighteenth and nineteenth centuries but we do know that it underwent several structural alterations in the twentieth century. The first of these occurred in 1927 when the facade of the old inn was changed. By the 1950s, on the ground floor,

*A VJ (victory over Japan) party held at the **George and Dragon** in August 1945. Fifty years later landlady Dorothy Reynolds, organised a reunion to commemmorate the earlier event. (Southwell Civic Society)*

there were two separate public rooms at the front, with kitchen and living quarters behind. In addition, there was a 'Tea Room' made available on certain occasions. Upstairs, as in many old inns, there was a big function room, often called the 'Buffs Room' because of its regular use by the local lodge of the Ancient Order of Buffaloes. Outside at the back, were the toilets and outbuildings including a wash house. In 1975 the inn was temporarily closed and refurbished. Then, in the 1980s, George and Dorothy Reynolds made substantial building changes. There were extensions completed at the back, with a bigger kitchen added and at the front the wall between the two rooms was knocked through, opening up that whole area. Later in the 1990s further refurbishing took place in a 'bistro' style.

Early activities. Back in the 1780s the *George and Dragon* and its publican, William Nicholson were well known for providing the headquarters for the Southwell Association for the Prosecution of Felons. With no professional or national system of policing before 1840, bringing offenders to justice was a slow, difficult and expensive business. This Southwell Association raised funds from the local gentry and prominent tradesmen and offered rewards to any person whose information would lead to the conviction of an offender. Apart from providing rooms for the regular meetings of the Association it would have been usual for possible offenders to be interrogated at the *George and Dragon.* William Nicholson, the innkeeper, was himself a member and clearly a leading light. We are very fortunate in having a substantial amount of information about the Association including the *1804 Rules and Orders booklet.* This rulebook tells us that '*each member should pay the customary subscription of two shillings and sixpence*'. Posters would be regularly shown outside the *George and Dragon* alerting local people as to what rewards they could expect to collect if they successfully 'apprehended' an offender. Note that in the case of an offender being found guilty of 'killing or maiming any Horse or..Sheep' they could face 'capital' punishment !

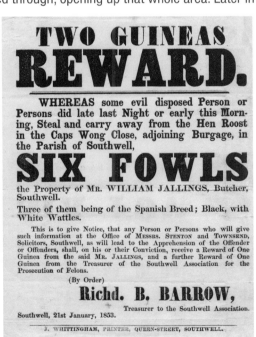

An 1853 'Reward' poster prepared by the Southwell Association for the Prosecution of Felons which had its headquarters at the George and Dragon. (NA DD/M/213/3)

The *George and Dragon* would also produce posters about specific offences and rewards for information given, as the poster, from 1853, shows. Despite the arrival on the national scene of local police forces in towns and rural areas, Southwell's Association was still functioning in 1867 as can be seen by the list of subscribers.[42] It is interesting to note how many family names still exist locally today. There seems to have been more local confidence in the Southwell Association for the Prosecution of Felons than there was for the newly appointed local police. A petition was presented in 1842 to the authorities as a protest against the new policing on the grounds that people didn't want to pay for its upkeep.[43] They were clearly much happier for the local gentry and businessmen to continue to subscribe to the Southwell Association.

We also have evidence that Southwell Musical Society regularly held its events in the public house from this obituary of the well known local historian, RP Shilton, that appeared in the *Nottingham and Newark Mercury* in August 1834.

> **N.N. Mercury–August 23 1834   Died**
> *Yesterday week, at Southwell, in his 76th year, Mr Richard Philips Shilton, an honest and much respected man, of great mental attainments, and author of the "Fall of Messina"(a poem), the "Histories of Southwell and Newark" and the "Battle of Stoke Field"... Mr Shilton commenced his professional career in the laudable work of schoolmaster, at Kirklington, then at Thurgarton and ultimately at Southwell always enjoying the praiseworthy estimation of both pupils and parents. The deceased was a a member of the musical society established by himself and three friends, in March 1786, and held at the George and Dragon, in Easthorpe. The members of this society attended the funeral, the last tribute of respect to one of their oldest members.*

Sales and auctions also took place at the *George and Dragon*. As early as December 1790 '*a Freehold Estate, situated in Easthorpe, consisting of four new brick and tile tenements ... in the possession of William and Elizabeth Birch, James Butler and Thomas Shepherd*' was sold at the public house. A further example is shown below.

*An auction at the **George and Dragon** in 1842. (NA DD/M 71/221)*

Like many public houses, the *George and Dragon* was also used, in its earlier years, as a venue for creditors' meetings. In the *Nottingham Journal* of February 9th 1793 we are told that '*the creditors of the late William Parr are desired to meet at the house of William Nicholson to receive their dividends.*'

Wartime and post-war memories. At this time Vincent Johnson-Cooper's family ran the pub and his father was in the army. His grandmother would arrange for parcels to be sent off to soldiers serving abroad and Geoff Dodsworth remembers being a grateful beneficiary of those parcels. When he was in France with the Sherwood Foresters Geoff said he received regular parcels consisting of 20 cigarettes, usually 'Players', a handkerchief, some food and a balaclava. The Johnson-Coopers had photographs of all the Southwell men and women who were abroad with the armed services pinned up on the walls. Sarah at this time laid on free 'Tripe Suppers', in the Tea Room. Throughout the war, local women used the *George* for knitting socks for soldiers. In August 1945 a lavish celebration took place at the inn when there was a 'Victory over Japan' street party held there. Fifty years later the landlady, Dorothy Reynolds, held a nostalgic party to commemorate the 1945 celebrations with former prisoner of war, Charlie Martin, invited as guest of honour.

Some years earlier the public house was used as the temporary incident room for a murder enquiry. A seventeen year old local girl, Karen Jane Waters, was found dead at her home adjacent to the public house, as reported by the *Newark Advertiser* on November 6 1985.

> **Murder!**
> *POLICE launched a murder inquiry after a 17 year old Southwell girl was found dead at her home in the village. Karen Jane Waters, was found in her Church Street flat just after 5-30pm yesterday by her common-law husband, farm labourer, Adam Everson. It is believed she had been raped and strangled and also had stab wounds to the chest.*
> **Raised the alarm**
> *Barbara Allen, the landlady of the neighbouring Bramley Apple public house, raised the alarm after the body was found. Police set up a temporary incident at the pub, where Karen was a customer.*

A further source of interest has been the unexplained happenings down in the cellars and in the upstairs rooms at dead of night. According to Vincent Johnson-Cooper there were many occasions when he would go down to the cellar to change a barrel only to find on his return to the bar that the pumps wouldn't work. Returning to the cellar he would find that 'someone' had removed the peg! A further unexplained happening was reported by landlords, Dorothy and George Reynolds in the

1980s when they would hear the strains of a violin and organ in the early hours of the morning, even though the organ and pianos had been removed from the inn several years before. A former landlord William Vince Johnson - Cooper had played the violin for many years but he died back in the 1950s!

Landlords. Mention has already been made of William Nicholson, publican c.1780- 1815, who played host to the prestigious Southwell Association for the Prosecution of Felons. He was clearly a very influential figure in the town as he was also a joiner and carpenter. Shilton's *History of Southwell* shows William Nicholson to be a public spirited man and quite wealthy. In 1794 he gave a generous contribution to the fund for raising a corps of local cavalry then ten years later enlisted himself in the *Loyal Southwell Volunteer Infantry.* [44] Two long serving families of publicans were the Woodwards (c.1825-1867) and the Stouts (c.1880-1908). Francis Stout was also a saddler.

Pride of place for the most long serving family, however, goes to the Johnson-Coopers. The grandparents of Vincent Johnson-Cooper ran the *George* from 1923 to 1972, almost five decades! According to Vincent his grandmother, Sarah, was a non-drinker whilst his grandfather,William, had a keen taste for beer. Sarah used to get suspicious when Vincent's grandfather went down to the cellar to change the barrels. As a way of checking he wasn't using the opportunity to have a quick drink, she insisted on his whistling from when he descended to the cellar to when he returned. According to Geoff Dodsworth, Sarah was a strong character and enjoyed giving orders to her husband. Geoff recalls several regulars of the *George and Dragon* mischievously greeting the landlord with, *'Good Evening George. How's the dragon?'* After grandfather died, Sarah wished to continue the business, but in those days the brewery insisted that because there were so much heavy work involved in running a public house there must be a man living in. To satisfy this regulation Vincent's father, who ran the *Hearty Goodfellow* down the road, arranged for Vincent to live at the *George* and help with changing the barrels and other jobs – he was 11 years old!

Brewery link. Beer would have been brewed on the premises in the early years but in the late nineteenth century several Newark breweries bought many of Southwell's public houses. The *George* became a Warwick and Richardson house until the 1970s, when first John Smiths Ltd. and then later Courage took over the brewery. In 1975 Courage closed the public house, selling it to Charles Chitton for £7,500 . He refurbished it and renamed it the *Bramley Apple*, after Southwell's famous apple.

A photograph of Sarah Johnson- Cooper with grandchildren, Vincent and Delia, taken in the 1950s. Sarah and William Johnson-Cooper were long-serving landlords.
(Vincent Johnson-Cooper)

Crown

Situation. The *Crown* Inn is situated on the corner of the Old Market Place and Church Street. It is one of the town's oldest inns and dates back to at least the early eighteenth century. Around 1820 when the inn was owned by the Chapter of Southwell Minster the front of the inn was substantially rebuilt. The high status that the inn enjoyed is shown by the entry in Pigot's *Commercial Directory* (1828), which noted that 'two very excellent inns are in this town- the *Crown Hotel* and the *Saracen's Head.*' The area around the *Saracen's Head* and the *Crown* - the Old Market Place - would at that time, have been the commercial hub of the town.

Crown Inn , Old Market Place (Terry Pearce)

Description. Apart from the reference to *'stables and other extensive outbuildings'* at the back, the sale notice, featured below, interestingly refers to the *'shops attached'* at the front of the inn. The frontage of many inns in the eighteenth century would have incorporated shops, some being permanent, others temporary stalls. As can be seen from the print on page 6, before its rebuilding around 1820 the *Crown* had a jettied first floor, supported by columns. At ground level, apart from the shops belonging to a grocer, saddler and glover, there would almost certainly have been a butcher's, as there was a slaughterhouse in the nearby yard.

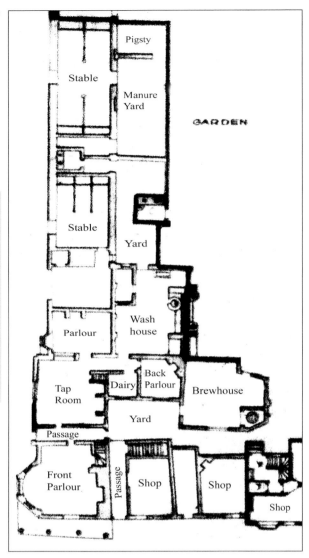

The old layout of the **Crown** from architect Richard Ingleman's 1819 plan. (NA Acc 7251)

> *NJ – November 20 1819* **To be Sold by Auction**
> *All that accustomed Public House, known by the Sign of the Crown Inn situate in the Centre of the Market Place; now occupied by Mr.W.Smith: together with Stables and other extensive Outbuildings, capable of great improvement and easily converted into a capital Inn, Hotel or Posting House.*
> *Also all those tenements or dwellings together with Shops attached.. now in occupation of Mr.W.Jallings, Grocer, Mr.G.Hawksley, Saddler and Mr.R.Thompson, Glover. Plans may be inspected at the office of Mr Ingleman.*

As an inn that counted the gentry and business classes amongst its clientele, the *Crown* after 1820 would have had a number of rooms on the ground floor available for business meetings and dining. On the first floor for many years there was a 'long room' that could be used for conducting sales but which could also serve as the inn's Assembly or Ballroom, valuable for dances, parties and special occasions. As it was an inn, the *Crown* would have accommodation available for travellers and business people on the first and second floors, and in the trade directories of the period it is interesting to note that the *Crown* marketed itself as a *Family and Commercial Hotel.*

The layout of the *Crown* has changed substantially over the years. Gwen Towers recalls the Assembly Room upstairs still being regularly used in the 1960s for weddings and private parties. Robert Beckett vividly remembers the 'dumb waiter' that worked between ground and first floors. At that time on the ground floor there would be a number of separate rooms, starting with the public bar and the residents' dining room immediately to the right of the main door. The bishop and clergy from Southwell Minster would often dine there. To the left of the main entrance was the smoke room and behind that was the tap room, which had swing doors and was very much separated off. In the 1970s structural alterations took place opening up the whole ground floor area.

Early commercial activities. The inn played a leading role in the town's commercial development. A very busy coaching inn, the *Crown* was on several major routes in the period 1820-45 including:

Names of Coaches	Coaching Routes	Names of Coaches	Coaching Routes
Tally-Ho	Lincoln-Manchester	Celerity	Barton-Nottingham
Champion	Lincoln-Manchester	Imperial	Hull-Nottingham
Accommodation	Newark-Nottingham	Royal Mail	Newark-Mansfield
Hark Forward	Lincoln-Buxton		

Not only did coaches stop at the inn, but its yard also served the village carriers. Trade directories inform us that local carriers Benjamin Revill and Henry Fern used the *Crown* inn-yard for their regular services to Newark, Nottingham and Mansfield.[45] With so many travellers requiring food and accommodation, the inn and its yard would have been one of the most lively and bustling locations in town.

The *Crown* was also extremely active in its earlier years holding sales and auctions on its premises. Before the general establishment of estate agencies and auction houses, the 'long room' of the larger town inns would serve as an auction house or general bazaar. All manner of sales took place there, from houses, farms and windmills to silver, antique books, furniture and carpets. As early as September 23rd 1769 we learn of the sale of a '*Farm at the house of William Randolph, Sign of the Crown*'. In the same newspaper on September 17th 1808 '*A Post Wind-Mill, eligibly sited in the town of Southwell,...in excellent repair...was to be sold at the Crown Hotel*'. Twenty years later a '*Sale of splendid Derbyshire Porcelain*' took place in the long room, being described as '*rare china, gratifying to the admirers of the fine art*'.[46] The inn was also the venue on May 10 1823 of the sale of the *White Lion* in Easthorpe.

SOUTHWELL COCKING.

NOTICE is hereby given, that there will be a Main of sixteen Cocks, fought at the Red Preband, Southwell, on the 15th Day of April, 1782, for a Mare, or Ten Pounds in Money value. Each Subscriber to put in Half a Guinea and the Winner to pay to the second best Twenty Shillings, and to the Third and Fourth Cock Ten Shillings each. No Cock to exceed the Weight of Four Pounds Six Ounces. The first Pair of Cocks to be on the Pit at Twelve o'Clock. To Fight in Silver.

*** A genteel Ordinary will be provided at the CROWN.
STATHEM and
GOODWIN, FEEDERS.

*Cock fighting held near the **Crown**, with 'A genteel ordinary' (meal) provided there afterwards. (NJ April 6 1782)*

Early social activities. Not only would commerce attract people to the inn but it was also a centre for sporting activities. Crowds of local people and visitors would be drawn to any inn that could put on popular events such as wrestling and cock-fights. These particular events drew crowds from every level of society and often led to frenzied betting. We have evidence that the inn regularly promoted both wrestling and cockfighting. In his 1781 diary, George Hodgkinson recorded, '*Adjourned to Taylor's (Crown) where the Gentlemen had engaged a room in order to see the wrestling match when one Whitworth of Farnsfield won the capital prize and Andrew Cooke of our parish, came in second. An immense quantity of spectators from all parts at the diversion*'.[47] Oral evidence suggests that Cooke's Lane, off Oxton Road, was named after this legendary prize fighter. Arguably though, the greatest sporting attraction of the day was to be found at a cockfighting match, where pairs of cocks would be set against one other in bloody fights to the death. The newspaper reference above shows a cock fight, with large sums of money involved, taking place in April 1782 opposite the *Crown* at the Red Prebend (demolished) with a meal to follow at the inn.

The inn-yard was also the venue for travelling theatrical shows, jugglers and acrobats. George Hodgkinson recalls how he '*Called at Stenton's .... all going to see the exhibition of Messrs. Daniel and Co. Taylor's (the Crown). Adjourned from Cade's about seven to the above entertainment and was much pleased with his deception at cards*'.[48]

Another regular activity at the *Crown*, as one of the most fashionable town inns, would have been the formal dinners for the local gentry and for official bodies like the Officers of the Southwell Regiment of Loyal Volunteers. The inn also hosted dinners on special 'patriotic' occasions such as in 1821 when King George IV's Coronation was celebrated.

> *NJ – July 28 1821* **Southwell Dinner**
> **to Celebrate Coronation of the King**
> *Throughout the whole length of the street front the inhabitants of Southwell celebrated the coronation with a dinner of ROAST BEEF, PLUM PUDDING, ALE and other requisites. The King's health was drunk with the utmost enthusiasm and the repeated cheering made the welkin ring again. Buns and pence were distributed to 800 children. There were also dinners at the Crown Inn and two of the other inns for the 'respectable inhabitants', traders and farmers ....so that the festival was observed by all ranks and degrees.*

Unlike the *Saracen's Head*, which seemed to cater solely for the leisured classes, the *Crown* did encourage the skilled working men to hold meetings and attend functions there. It was quite common for working men to meet as a 'club' at inns, often as a friendly, benefit or charitable society. There were two groups in particular which regularly chose the inn as their favoured venue, the Hop Growers Society and the Friendly Society of Gentlemen Florists. A typical notice appeared in the *Nottingham Journal* on August 9 1788. '*The Hop Growers and Dealers in Hops in pursuance of their first meeting are happy to inform the public that a very respectable company of the above met at the house of William Keeton, at the Crown Inn, Southwell. NB. Mr William Handley and Mr William Sketchley are subscribers to the meeting*'.

A meeting of the Friendly Society of Gentlemen Florists. (NJ April 13 1782)

Post-war memories. Roland and Gwen Towers recall that middle-aged couples made up a substantial percentage of the regular clientele in the 1960s. It was still seen as one of the top hotels in the region and Gwen Towers can remember the Bishop of Southwell frequently making dinner reservations in the Residents' Dining Room for himself and his party. Herbert Lewin remembers the Special Constabulary using the upstairs Assembly Room for dinners. Robert Beckett and Dennis Broomfield recall that at weekends there was always waiter service only in the various bars and small rooms downstairs. Geoff Dodsworth recalls the British Legion meeting in the Smoke Room. The tap room, off Church Street, was regularly full of the staff from J.H. Kirkby's, the family grocer, across the road. It also attracted plenty of local characters. One particular incident that occurred there is still vividly remembered by a number of people. Billy Burrows, the Rag and Bone man, who lived off Lower Kirklington Road where he had a scrap yard, had sneaked into the Tap Room, leaving his faithful horse waiting patiently in the *Crown* yard. Landlady Kitty Hall went over and said to him, *'Billy, I don't mind you coming in as long as you clear up the 'mess' your old horse leaves !'*

'Alright Mrs.,' replied Billy Burrows. Next time Billy came into the Crown he went straight up to Kitty Hall commenting *'I've sorted horse out, Mrs, I've tied top coat to horse's backside so it won't make a mess.'* Billy Burrows had come up with an original solution to the problem!

Innkeepers. A number of the earlier innkeepers used the Nottingham newspapers to inform the public that they were now 'in residence' at the *Crown*. A typical entry was the following.

NJ - April 3 1779 Robert Taylor
most respectfully acquaints his friends and the public in general that he has taken upon the Crown Inn which he has now fitted up in a new elegant manner, where he hopes for a continuation of favours of those gentlemen who have used the same inn

Eight years later, in November 1787, Robert Taylor was followed at the *Crown* by Samuel Keeton, who immediately publicised that he *'had laid in a large stock of Foreign Wines and Spirits'* and *'exerted his utmost endeavours to render the Accommodation as genteel as possible.'*[49] One year later Samuel Keeton took the opportunity of informing the general public that *'as the Cross Keys Inn was temporarily shut up, he humbly solicits such who frequented the house to make trial of the Crown Inn'*. Clearly Mr Keeton set out to be a true entrepreneur, but sadly the business did not expand as he had hoped as a few years later there is a short notice in the *Nottingham Journal* to the effect that Mr Keeton had gone bankrupt and had *'handed over his effects to Mr William Smith and Mr W Handley'*.[50]

In 1820 the innkeeper was William Smith, who received permission from the Minster Chapter to make structural alterations, resulting in the building we see today. From the *Life of John Holmes* we learn that William Smith was talking to a local Southwell man, Mr Shelton, about future events. Mr. Shelton commented that he was sure the innkeeper would die on a certain day in the year 1850. The innkeeper replied *'I never believe such things'*. When this day arrived, William Smith happened to be in Nottingham at a time when cholera was rife in the town. He was suddenly taken seriously ill and, remembering the warning, asked his friends to take him home to Southwell so he could die there. John Holmes concludes, *'He did die that day and was buried that night and a lot of lime was thrown in his grave as the gentry of Southwell was afraid he had brought the cholera into the town'.*[51] Henry and Sarah Sharp ran the inn for the best part of forty years from c1860-1900. Henry Sharp, apart from his work as a publican, was also postmaster and cab proprietor.

Into the twentieth century we find innkeeper John Tatham in 1924 hauled in front of the Southwell magistrates and fined £2 for selling intoxicating liquor during prohibited hours. Finally, there are many people today who have fond memories of Stan and Kitty Hall who ran the *Crown* in the late 1970s.

The *Crown* would have brewed its own beer until the late 1800s but by that date it was increasingly difficult for inns to avoid being taken over by a big brewery. In the early twentieth century the Chapter of Southwell Minster sold the inn to Hornby's Ltd, a subsidiary of the Mansfield Brewery.

Dumbles

Early history. The *Dumbles*, for most of its existence called the *Lord Nelson*, is situated in Westhorpe close to the junction with Allenby Road. Despite its recent change of name, many Westhorpe people still affectionately refer to the old inn as the *Nellie*. There has been a public house on this site since the mid 1700s and in the early 1800s we know that the inn took the name of the national hero, Horatio Nelson, following his great naval victories at the Nile and later Trafalgar. We cannot be certain what the inn was called before it became the *Admiral Nelson*, but it is possible that it was the *Red Lion*. By the 1820s the inn was more usually referred to as the *Lord Nelson*, when the hero was posthumously honoured with an hereditary title.

*The **Lord Nelson** in the early twentieth century. (Southwell Civic Society)*

Description. A deed dated June 7 1862, between Thomas Woodward, maltster and publican, and Edward Hall, describes the property being surrendered as, *'All that messauge or tenement now used as a public house called the Admiral Lord Nelson with the yard garden, stables, outbuildings and premises'*. It had a traditional layout with two main rooms downstairs – a bar room and a smoke room – and a large room upstairs for functions. I have spoken to many local people about the *Lord Nelson* in the 1940-75 period and they remember the *Nellie* as having a very smart lounge bar (the smoke room) with an upstairs function room that was often used for childrens' parties. Robert Beckett speaks of the *Nellie* in the 1960s as 'the *Saracen's Head* of Westhorpe' in that it had an air of respectability and comfort that at the time many public houses lacked. In the 1950s and 1970s Newark and Southwell Magistrate Court licensing records tell us that structural alterations resulted in extending the premises and removing some interior walls to create a more open feel.

Early commercial and administrative activities. The *Lord Nelson* was a centre for the carrying and coaching trades in the early nineteenth century. Trade directories indicate that the 'Champion' coach, travelling from Lincoln to Nottingham, stopped at the *Lord Nelson* at 9am and 5pm. The coaching trade would have been a very useful supplement to the landlord's income. The inn was also used as a venue for inquests. The *Newark Advertiser* of August 25 1855 reports, *'INQUEST at the home of Mrs. Anne Woodward, the Lord Nelson, on the body of Mrs Ann Ward widow 66 years – found dead at her home.'* Like many other town inns the *Lord Nelson* held auctions of properties on its premises, as the following newspaper extract shows.

A 1960s postcard of the lounge bar. (Anne Loveridge)

NJ - March 26 1814 **To Be Sold By Auction**
at the House of Mr Bush, the Admiral Nelson, Westhorpe A substantial, well built Brick and Tiled House, containing three rooms on the ground floor, three good Lodging rooms and two Attics together with a capital brick and tiled barn, stable, Dovecote and other outbuildings and the Homestead containing one acre of excellent grassland. Particulars see Mr James Baily of Halam.

Social activities in recent times. For many years there were table skittles in the bar and outside, a croquet lawn. Landlords were also in the habit of encouraging groups of cyclists to visit and stay overnight. Many of its activities over the years have been focused on the immediate community around Westhorpe and Westgate. Arthur Frecknall remembers the regular local flower shows in the 1950s and 60s whilst Ann Loveridge, sister of landlady Mary Breedon, has strong memories of many private parties that used the function room upstairs. Ann and her sister enjoyed doing the catering for these events. Yvonne and Harry Cooling look back with some pleasure at the Saturday night musical evenings with Alf Rodgers often leading the singing and Mick Hall playing the organ. Mary West recalls the Folk Club sessions on Sunday nights, run by June Loughton, which included some distinguished folk singers as Jake Thackray. The local Gardening Club usually met at the *Nellie*, and in the function room upstairs Robert Beckett recalls that the Buffaloes Lodge regularly held their meetings. There would be the annual bus trip of *Nellie* regulars to the Grand National, and the visits by Morris Dancers are fondly remembered by local people. Yvonne Cooling still has vivid memories of the fun they all had at the Easter Bonnet Parades and Anne Loveridge remembers how busy the *Nellie* would suddenly become when a coach, bound either for the East Coast or the Racecourse, stopped for refreshments. In the 1970s Westhorpers became very concerned about the proposed demolition of rows of old cottages and so a local conservation group was formed to fight the cause. Meetings took place at the *Nellie*.

Public Meeting
to discuss the conservation and improvement of Westhorpe
On Wednesday, 31st March 1971 at 8pm. All are invited to attend.

Innkeepers. The Woodward family had a long relationship, as innkeepers, with the *Lord Nelson* from c.1825 -63. Thomas Woodward was shown in deeds of property transfer and in trade directories as being a maltster as well as a publican. His wife, Anne Woodward, continued as publican when Thomas died in the early 1850s. In more recent times another family team, first George then Gladys Newton, ran the *Nellie* from 1934 to 1963. Harry Cooling remembers that George Newton was tragically killed, when he was involved in a road traffic accident on the A614 after visiting Doncaster Races.

Originally the *Lord Nelson* would have brewed its own beer but by the late nineteenth century, like many other town inns, it became a tied house. Early in the 1900s the Askew Ball Brewery of Alfreton supplied the beer. Later, in the interwar period, the James Shipstone Brewery took over the *Nellie*, to be followed by James Hole, one of the two big Newark breweries. This link with Newark remained until 1974.

The Hearty Goodfellow today (Terry Pearce)

Hearty Goodfellow

Early history. The *Hearty Goodfellow* is situated on the boundary of Church Street and Easthorpe, opposite Farthingate. The name of this public house is taken from a once popular ballad in the 1860s, *'I am a hearty goodfellow, I live at my ease; I work when I am willing, I play when I please'.*

The *Hearty*, as it is commonly referred to, seems to invite rhymes as this wording from a 1960s marketing card shows. *'When things go wrong and the world seems blue, Listen to what I'm telling you, All the World will be bright and mellow, After a drink at the Hearty Goodfellow.'* We have records to show that there was an inn on the site in the late eighteenth century.[52] The building could have been even older as local people speak of the *Hearty* being a recruiting centre for the Royal Marines, at a time when the country was at war with France. The *Hearty* today possesses a large, attractive garden which slopes down to the stream behind the inn. A newspaper notice dating back to March 1817 gives a description of the inn.

NJ –March 22 1817 **To Let**
All that good accustomed public house known by the name of the HEARTY GOODFELLOW; together with large Orchard and Garden Stables, Piggeries and other necessary Outbuildings now in the occupation of Mr.John Frier who will quit at Lady Day or May Day next...The above will be let either Yearly or for a term of Years as may be agreed upon. Enquire of Mr.Jenkinson, Maltster, Southwell.

There have been substantial alterations over the years but, even if today the *Hearty* may be said to have lost much of its historic appearance, the inside retains a feel of genuine age. According to John Luckhurst, whose grandparents, Albert and Clara Sophie Luckhurst, ran the *Hearty* in the early twentieth century, there were originally two separate rooms, a'tap' room and a 'smoke' room with a 'jug and bottle' (serving hatch) in the centre. This hatch gave immediate access for members of the public, who didn't want to drink in the pub, and allowed them to take bottles or jugs of beer away. In later years structural alterations were made which resulted in the opening up of the front rooms. In those earlier years, John Luckhurst recalls that the beer would be brought up from the cellars in big enamel jugs, as 'pumps' had not yet arrived on the scene. At the back of the property there were always plenty of outbuildings, many of them originally stables, and in the orchard another large, brick building. Publicans over the years would have been very happy to make profitable use of the piggeries, allotments and orchard as a way of supplementing their basic income.

Early social and commercial activities. In the mid nineteenth century the *Hearty* was selected on a number of occasions as a venue for inquests. This was quite a common practice at the time. Publicans would be expected to provide an appropriate room for the reception of any unfortunate person, who had met an unexplained death. The publicans at the *Hearty* would ordinarily not receive any remuneration for letting out their rooms '*but they would have been only too aware that additional revenue, in the form of post-inquest eating, would invariably be forthcoming.*'[53] One such inquest at the *Hearty* occurred on January 19th 1856 when, according to the *Newark Advertiser*, '*at the home of Mr.Revill, the Hearty Goodfellow in Easthorpe, there will take place an inquest on the body of a child of six months*'. Another use of the public house at this time was as a venue for holding creditors' meetings in situations when a local person had been declared bankrupt or had died. In the *Nottingham Journal* of the 22nd June, we learn that there was to be a '*Creditors Meeting at the house of Joshua Brown, the Hearty Goodfellow, Easthorpe*'. Sales and auctions of houses, shops and other property also took place at the *Hearty* in the nineteenth century, when there was a marked absence of public buildings such as auction rooms and estate agencies. The example shown is especially interesting as it shows the contemporary agricultural character of Easthorpe with the sale of a local blacksmith's shop.

Activities at the *Hearty* in more recent years. Geoff Dodsworth remembers Christmas 1937 when he and a friend became of age to go and drink in a pub. Loaded with the mighty sum of 6d each they decided to try their luck at the *Hearty*. A soon as they walked in they saw that the rooms had been set out for a huge Christmas Party. Landlord and regulars had been saving up for some time to supply this mighty feast. Despite this Geoff and friend were made doubly welcome and had a great night. Because of the friendliness they decided to make the *Hearty* their regular call. According to John Luckhurst and Vincent Johnson-Cooper, excursion buses to Skegness in the 1960s, would regularly make use of the excellent car park. Coachloads of travellers with forty minutes drinking time, would pile into the pub with bar staff given clear instructions to have the pints all ready. Also at this time, the Southwell Amateurs would use the *Hearty* as a changing room for their football matches on the War Memorial Park. Charlie Martin, a regular, was involved in the organisation. A further feature of the post war years was that publicans in the 1950s would open up as early as 6-00 am to offer breakfasts to the local people doing shiftwork at Carey's, the Southwell Lace Factory. Many Lace Factory workers were regulars, including Arthur Chamberlain, the chief engineer. A little later in the 1960s, when the large farm on Church Street was demolished and the Farthingate development took place, Vincent Johnson-Cooper recalls his mother, the publican, being hard pressed all day with construction workers wanting drinks.

BLACKSMITH'S SHOP AND PREMISES.
EASTHORPE, SOUTHWELL.
ELIGIBLE SITUATION FOR AN INVESTMENT.

TO BE SOLD BY AUCTION.
On Monday, the 25th of November, 1833, at Five, for Six o'Clock in the Evening, at the House of Mr. Samuel Revill, the Hearty Good Fellow Inn, at Easthorpe aforesaid, subject to such Conditions as will be then agreed on unless previously disposed of by Private Contract, of which due Notice will be given,

ALL those TWO DWELLING HOUSES, in the several occupations of Messrs JOHN and MATTHEW REVILL, with excellent Gardens behind the same, and Yard, Blacksmith's Shop, and Shoeing Hovel adjoining, in front thereof, the whole situate in Easthorpe, in the Town of Southwell aforesaid, and on the High Road leading from Newark to Mansfield and Nottingham.

Also, to be disposed of the Good Will of an old established and most excellent Business as a Blacksmith, now carried on on the Premises, by the said John Revill, who is declining the same.

Immediate Possession will be given of the House in his occupation, and of the Shop, Shoeing Hovel, and one of the Gardens.—The Purchaser to take the Stock in Trade and Tools at a fair valuation.

The whole of the Premises are Copyhold, of the Manor of Southwell, and the fine is small and certain. The Buildings are in a good state of Repair.

For further particulars application may be made to Messrs BARROW and SON, Solicitors, Southwell, or to SAMUEL REVILL, at the above named inn, and who will show the Premises. [Southwell, 5th Nov. 1833]

An auction of a blacksmith's shop in Easthorpe at the Hearty. (NNM November 16 1833)

Many innkeepers kept pigs as a useful extra source of income and Vincent's father was no exception. Vincent recalls that his father won a skittles competition at a local garden party. The prize turned out to be a piglet (named Rupert) which was subsequently reared on the bottle and then exchanged for a another pig, (Penny) that could have a litter. Vincent remembers his father's delight following the arrival of 91 pigs after 16 litters! Arthur Merrin, the 'Pigman' would then see that the pigs were taken to the market to provide extra income for the publican. To keep the pigs fed, Arthur Merrin would take his tractor and trailer round the town collecting swill from, among other places, the Fish and Chip shop, Brackenhurst Farm and Caudwell House. The piggery at the back of the Hearty became so extensive that it occupied virtually the whole of the garden area that we see today.

Hearty regulars in the Tap Room during the early 1960s. Left to right: Arthur Merrin (the 'Pig Man'), M King, R Taylor, J Taylor, J Rushby, D Rushby, F Johnson-Cooper, J Boucher, W Boucher, Vincent Johnson-Cooper, Vera Johnson-Cooper, K Peet, J Davis, R Haywood. (Vincent Johnson-Cooper)

Well known characters. 'Matty' Grundy was a character who stands out in the memories of John Luckhurst and Vincent Johnson-Cooper. Otherwise known as 'Andy Capp', Matty was well known for his tap dancing routines. He also fancied himself as a boxing champion, particularly after a few drinks. John Luckhurst recalls that one night after closing time Matty Grundy, on his way home, took on an evergreen tree! Two other 'characters' were 'Chippy' Greaves and 'Jumper' Bartlett who habitually moved round most of the town's 'pubs', mainly because they kept on getting banned at various times. Another regular at the *Hearty* was the 'Rag and Bone' man, Billy Burrows, who always enjoyed a glass or two of Guinness. Billy would take his horse and cart and stop at most of the Church Street pubs on his way round the town, collecting cardboard and other items. Several people can recall seeing the poor old horse waiting patiently outside the *Hearty* for its owner to return. According to Geoff Dodsworth you could always tell Billy's horse because its stomach was almost dragging on the floor. Billy, an ex-Minster Grammar School pupil, was instantly recognised by his trilby hat, black coat and wellington boots, where he allegedly kept all his money!

Landlords. Many of the *Hearty* publicans had multiple jobs, following the common practice then of the publican's wife running the pub whilst the husband worked at his other employment. Early in the 1820s Joshua Brown, who had been a joiner, was followed by Samuel Revill who was a hop grower. In the 1890s William Foster was a bootmaker, whilst Albert Lukehurst in the early 1900s worked also as a property dealer. The Lukehursts' successor, Harry May, had a coal merchant's business in the period between the wars. He was also a District Councillor for twelve years and later his son Albert May served for many years on the parish council.

Secondly, there was a tradition of long serving families of publicans at the *Hearty*. In the nineteenth century Samuel, Matthew and William and Mary Revill had run the public house for the best part of fifty years from 1830-80. In the twentieth century, Albert and Clara Lukehurst had been tenants from 1906-28 Their daughter Kathleen married Harry May and they ran the house from 1928 to 1954. Finally, another well known local family, the Johnson-Coopers, who ran the *George and Dragon* up the road, were the tenants from 1954-72.

Beer would have been brewed on the premises in the early years, but by the late nineteenth century the larger Nottinghamshire breweries had bought out most of the public houses in Southwell. William Allen's, Worksop and Retford Brewery, had ownership of the *Hearty* from the1890's until the 1970s. It then became a Whitbread house in the 1980s.

Newcastle Arms

Early history. The *Newcastle Arms* was built in the early 1860s to provide refreshment and accommodation for passengers and tradesmen using the Southwell railway station, hence its situation on Station Road or, as it was then known, Burgage North. Southwell was connected to the Midland Railway network in July 1847 with a short branch line from Rolleston Junction on the Nottingham–Lincoln line. There was not a regular passenger service by steam locomotives, however, until 1860. The line was extended westwards to Mansfield in April 1871 with stations built at Kirklington, Farnsfield and Rainworth.

In the nineteenth century the *Newcastle Arms* was also known as the *Commercial and Family Hotel*. The inn was named after the owners of Clumber Park, the Dukes of Newcastle, who had great influence in the region but owned no land in Southwell that we are aware of. Beer might well have been brewed on the premises in the early years but by the1890s the inn had been tied to James Shipstone and Sons of New Basford, Nottingham and until recently it remained a Shipstone house. Many local people still refer to the pub as *Bob Hall's*, after the landlord who kept it for fifty years (1904-55).

Memories of *Bob Hall's*. 'Jock' Grant has two clear memories of Bob Hall, the long serving landlord. Bob was a very short man and as the bar was quite high he had to stand on a box to serve customers. In the days before pumps had been introduced, Jock has vivid memories of Bob Hall constantly going down to the cellars and bringing back beer in big jugs. Geoff Dodsworth first visited *Bob Hall's* in 1939 before he was sent to France with the Sherwood Foresters. Training was at the Drill Hall on Newark Road and he and his mates would be on patrol in the woods nearby before reporting to Permanent Staff Instructor Whittle, who could be reliably located at *Bob Hall's!* According to Geoff the Shipstone's beer at *Bob Hall's* was powerful stuff, an acquired taste, and was often referred to as 'fighting beer'. He recalls one fight outside the pub when two over seventies were arguing about their respective military service. 'Jumper' Bartlett, who had been in the Sherwood Rangers Yeomanry and who always took his paybook around with him in a bag as proof of his service record, became very violent when Joe Covell raised doubts about 'Jumper's' military career. The spirited fight that followed was finally broken up when the father of John Pitchford sorted them out! Apparently 'Jumper' and Joe shook hands and immediately got back to drinking Shipstone's 'fighting beer' together. Malcolm Greaves remembers 'Jumper', a very capable darts player, always looking out for someone less skilled than him to have a game and a bet with.

During the Second World War there were two troops of soldiers based in the Southwell area; the Essex Yeomanry and the Household Cavalry (the Guards). Nancy Harrison recalls that some of them were billeted at *Bob Hall's*. She remembers her father earnestly telling her, *'Nancy, don't have anything to do with the Guards! Stick to the Yeomanry!'*

*A group of people about to board the train around the turn of the century. The **Newcastle Arms** was built primarily to provide refeshments and accommodation for railway passengers. (Southwell Civic Society)*

Outing From The Newcastle Arms

*A group of regulars from the **Newcastle Arms** on a day's outing. Landlord, Bob Hall is on the front row. (Philip Robinson)*

Geoff Dodsworth also remembers vividly the gas lights fitted on the walls. Another feature of these years was the regular sing-song with resident pianist. Frequent users of the inn were the members of Sherwood Rifle Club and trout fishermen on the River Greet. David Hutchinson recalls that the fishermen used to leave the fish at the pub. Obviously in the years before the station closed in 1959, local people using the railway would have been customers at the inn. According to Herbert Lewin one such group of regulars worked at Ransome and Marles bearing factory in Newark. They used the railway through the week but on Sundays, when there was no service, they walked to Fiskerton to catch the train to Newark. After the closure of the station, buses still used the *Newcastle Arms* as a terminus and David Hutchinson was frequently allowed to leave his bicycle at the inn before he took the bus to Nottingham.

Mr.Fox, a Normanton farmer, was remembered by some people for regularly coming on horseback to the inn and departing, usually very unsteadily, on his horse back to Normanton. Two other characters, remembered by David Hutchinson, were 'Jo'Smith and Bob Burrows. They had both been in the forces in the 1940s and on their return in the 1950s they had a special arrangement with Bob Hall, the landlord, to be given an enamel jug filled with ale to drink outside. According to local legend, Bob Burrows one night drank seventeen pints without going to the toilet.

*Outside the **Newcastle Arms** in the early years of the motor car. (Southwell Civic Society).*

Innkeepers. Francis and Robert Hall covered the entire period 1880–1955. Charlie Watts and Herbert Lewin remember that Bob Hall, as well as being a publican, also ran a horse drawn hearse and had a coal merchant's business, with stables in the yard for horse and dray. David Hutchinson and Jock Grant have memories of Bob Hall's son, Cecil Hall, who grazed his cows on the Burgage and milked them by hand. In the years between Bob Hall leaving the scene and John Lazenby taking over as publican, the *Newcastle Arms* was occasionally in trouble with the local magistrates. The publican received four separate fines for supplying intoxicating liquor during non-permitted hours. Licensing records inform us, too, that John Lazenby (1964-74) applied for and received authorisation for customers to play whist, solo and rummy as long as the stakes did not exceed two shillings and there were only four tables.

Old Coachhouse

*Inn sign of the **White Lion**..*

Early years. This old public house, until the 1990s known as the *White Lion*, is situated on the corner of Easthorpe, opposite the junction with Fiskerton Road. Its history goes back to the mid 1700s at least, though the first written reference we have is from the *1791 Universal Directory of Great Britain,* which states that amongst the traders of Southwell was a certain *'Daniel Cox, Victualler, White Lion'*.

Description of the property. Many public houses have changed so much in appearance over the years that they lose the sense of being an old building. But despite having major structural alterations in 1925 and further structural changes in the last fifteen years, the *Old Coach House* has very definitely retained the character of being an old public house. Its low ceilings and numerous little rooms give it a distinctive snug feel, especially in winter when the open fire is blazing. Equally, the furniture and the original old fireplace range give it an authentic alehouse look. The layout of the old pub suggests the interior character has slowly evolved rather than being artificially designed. Originally there were three small rooms close to the road which were available to the public. The area away from the roadside was private living quarters. The toilets were roughly in the same place as today but access was from the yard.

*The **White Lion** in 1905. Note the landlord's name, GW Foster, on the wall and the brewhouse behind. Hunts in those days would have been a common sight in the town. (Southwell Civic Society)*

Its external appearance has also retained much of its original character, though like many other public houses, land has been lost at the rear where there would have been a yard and outbuildings for waggons and horses. There is no record of coaches using the pub since the premises were unlikely to have been extensive enough, so it is somewhat surprising that the pub was renamed the *Old Coach House.* An early newspaper reference to an auction gives a good idea of the external layout.

> *NJ – May 10 1823* **To Be Sold By Auction**
> *A very desirable and well accustomed public house in Easthorpe known by the Sign of the White Lion, being the first public house at the entrance of the town.*

Changes in recent years. In the 1990s Steve Hussey bought the property and proceeded to make a number of changes. The private living quarters at the back were converted into a customer seating area. To give a greater feeling of age, plaster on the walls was taken off to show the old bricks. The name was changed to the *Old Coach House,* it became a Real Ale pub and young, welcoming staff were selected. These changes had a huge impact on the popularity of the pub. In the words of Dennis Broomfield, who has been a regular for over 30 years, '*After being a quiet drinking place where there were usually only about fifteen regulars, suddenly you found you couldn't get in the door!*' Dennis adds that the appeal of the *Old Coach House* also extended far and wide whereas before it had been purely a locals' pub. He summarised the huge transformation by saying that '*before the changes all the regulars knew everyone else whereas after the changes you could go in and not know a soul.*'

Post-war memories. Local Easthorpe residents have seen the pub as a place to meet friends, enjoy a drink and a game of cards, darts or dominoes. There have been for years mens' and ladies' darts teams and dominoes teams. In earlier times, meanwhile, there was the skittle alley in the backyard. Dennis Broomfield can plainly remember some of the better known locals over the years. Bob Ward, a very good amateur goalkeeper would stand at the bar and pass on plenty of football stories, whilst Edwin Cottam, a local blacksmith, was one for telling jokes and creating plenty of laughter. Another regular, who had played football until he was over fifty, was Charlie Martin. He then turned to coaching and managing teams. The pub has always had close links with the Easthorpe allotments with allotment holders often calling for a drink on their way back home. Meetings of the allotment holders often took place at the pub.

Landlords. The Cox family ran the house from c.1785 to 1830, followed later by William Smedley, whose service stretched from c.1860 to 1900. Best of all was the dedication of George and Euphemia Foster, who ran the pub from 1900 to 1958. Again several of the victuallers had other occupations, presumably to bolster the family income. This would usually entail leaving the house under the daytime supervision of the victualler's wife. Trade directories tell us that John Lynn in 1828 was also a baker, and, sixteen years later, Matthew Bramley followed a butcher's trade, whilst William Smedley was one of many boot and shoemakers in the town.

Brewery links. Originally the *White Lion* would have had a brewhouse which provided its own beer. There is evidence from a will of victualler William Smedley in 1887 that he has passed to his wife '*stock in trade and brewing utensils*'.[54] By the late nineteenth century, however, like many other small public houses, the *White Lion* would have found it hard to stay independent at a time when taxation had increased in the beer trade. The pub sold out to the Warwick and Richardson Brewery in Newark, who remained in control until the 1960s when they were taken over by John Smith of Tadcaster. In the 1970s they, in turn, were taken over by Courage Brewery. Currently the *Old Coach House* is a Free House.

Reindeer

Early history. This old inn, whose history goes back into the late eighteenth century, is situated on Westgate close to the junction with Nottingham Road. At the beginning of the nineteenth century, when the innkeeper was John Bauser, the *Reindeer* was at the forefront of many town activities. After 1810 little is heard of the inn until the 1840s when, following extensive alterations, there is evidence of a revival under the management of George Abbott. By the middle of the nineteenth century it had become one of the town's leading coaching inns.

As the 1811 newspaper advertisement shows, the earlier building was a sizeable property, with a number of bars and dining room on the ground floor, plenty of accommodation for travellers upstairs and a large yard with stabling for twelve horses.

*The **Reindeer Inn,** Westgate (Terry Pearce)*

A changed layout and design followed the rebuilding in the 1840s. According to a later auction advertisement from 1847, there was a *'brewhouse on site and excellent arched cellaring,'* which can still be admired today. Special mention was made of the inn's *'superior furnishings and the availability of Harvey's Rooms'.*[55] This may refer to the upstairs Assembly Room, which for many years was a popular attraction for locals and visitors and as late as the 1960s was used for family parties and musical evenings. Stabling provision had increased by 1847 to twenty horses and there was encouragement to any local trader who might wish to rent any of the innyard outbuildings. This was common in other town inns, where innkeepers would either rent or even carry on a trade there themselves, so adding to the innkeepers' earning power. Even after change of use of the outbuildings and despite structural alterations in the 1970s, the old inn-yard retains a strong sense of history.

BLACK BOY INN COACH OFFICE,
LONG-ROW, NOTTINGHAM.

NOTTINGHAM AND GAINSBOROUGH
Royal Perseverance.

THE Nobility, Gentry, and Public in general are respectfully informed, that a New LIGHT POST COACH, called the ROYAL PERSEVE- RANCE, will commence running on Monday next, the 22d Instant, and every following Morning (Sunday excepted), from the Black Boy Inn Coach Office, Long-row, Nottingham, to the Monson's Arms Inn, Gainsborough, by way of Southwell, Newark, and Lincoln, where it will arrive the same Afternoon ; and return every Morning (Sunday excepted) at Ten o'Clock, through the above-mentioned places, and arrive at the Black Boy Inn, Nottingham, the same Evening.   Performed by
JOHN WILMOTT, ROBERT EAST, GEO. ABBOTT, WM. NALL, and JOSEPH BAXTER.

Notice for the *'Royal Perseverance'* coach', one of many coaches that changed horses at local inns. (NNM April 13 1836)

Commercial activities. In the nineteenth century the *Reindeer* made a significant contribution to the commercial life of the town. The inn was an important stopping place on the coach routes from Newark to Nottingham. White's *1844 Trade Directory* states, '*COACHES from George Abbott's Reindeer – the 'Accommodation' from Newark to Nottingham, change horses here at eight in the morning and at half past seven in the evening'.*

With the coming of the railways innkeepers had to adapt their businesses to meet the new transport needs. The *Reindeer* publicans seemed to have successfully done this as we find in 1853 William Baker, who followed George Abbott, was laying on an 'omnibus' to meet every train at Fiskerton. This type of business activity had expanded further by 1864 when William Baker was described in a trade directory as a *'horse and gig letter, omnibus proprietor and agent to Midland Railway Company'.* The *Reindeer* was also the location for the '*Livery and Bate Stables*' in the town. Three years later *White's Directory* of 1872 stated that, apart from the *Reindeer* being a centre for the hire of horses, gigs and omnibuses, the inn was also a Posting House. Throughout the late Georgian and early Victorian periods the *Reindeer* used its large rooms for auctions and sales of various kinds. In 1808 *'a bakehouse in the Market Place, owner Mr.Rogers'* was up for auction. In the same year a horse, 'Patriot', was for sale at the inn. In 1812 Rudsey Farm was sold there and in the following year there was a number of sales of household effects.[56]

Post-war memories. People living today have strong memories of the *Reindeer* in the post-Second World War period. Robert Beckett recalls that the *Reindeer's* Assembly Room, upstairs, was frequently used for parties and dances. Keith Anker and Herbert Lewin remember Southwell St. Mary's football team, in the absence of a sports pavilion on the War Memorial Park, changing upstairs before they ran off for the game. Keith also has vivid memories of walking into the inn and seeing hams hanging on hooks from the beams for curing. Herbert Lewin recalls that farmers, staff and workers from Brackenhurst College have always been regular users of the *Reindeer.* One of these farmers, Mr Stephenson, would be in the inn yard with his horse and cart everyday at 12 noon and would return to farming at 2 o'clock precisely. The inn was also popular with cyclists as a regular watering hole.

Innkeepers. George Abbott and William Baker played major roles in the town's coaching and omnibus business. George Abbott was an extraordinary example of the Victorian entrepreneur – publican, postmaster, coach proprietor, livery stable keeper and even vetinerary surgeon! His successor, William Baker, was equally multi-skilled. As well as being a publican, he was a horse and gig proprietor and managed at the same time to be a farmer and agent to the Midland Railway Company. These two'legendary' figures dominated the scene from c1825 to 1875. Earlier John Bauser, innkeeper from 1810 to 1818, had been just as resourceful, witness the *Nottingham Journal,* which shows the *Reindeer,* in those years, regularly holding sales, auctions and public meetings. On his departure in September 1818 John Bauser put the following notice in that same paper,

> *Reindeer Inn* Southwell
> *John Bauser returns his most grateful thanks to the inhabitants*
> *of Southwell and the public for the many favours conferred on him during*
> *his eight years residence in the place and hopes by his attention to merit*
> *their future favours at the Angel Inn, Retford.*

This is a good example of what had become a common practice at the time – successful Southwell innkeepers looking to take on more challenging and potentially more lucrative posts at inns elsewhere. In the twentieth century the innkeeper with the longest service is Rebecca Downes who ran the inn from 1886 to 1927. Charlie Watts, in his discussions with Bob Hardstaff, remembers Rebecca Downes with fondness as his first teacher.

The *Reindeer* brewed its own beer for many years but, like most of the local public houses, faced rising costs by the turn of the nineteenth century. The pub became tied to W.S.Davy's Devon Brewery from Newark until 1920, when it was bought out by the Warwick and Richardson Brewery, also from Newark.

*A Warwick and Richardson Brewery token. The **Reindeer** was a Warwick pub from 1920-75.*

Saracen's Head

Early history. The *Saracen's Head*, situated in the Old Market Place in the centre of town, was at different times known as the *Turk's Head* and the *King's Arms*. A deed dating from October 20th 1396 recorded the transfer of the building from the Archbishop of York to John Fysher and his wife, giving evidence that the old inn's illustrious history goes back to mediaeval times, but that period is beyond the scope of this book. In 1670, only a few years after the celebrated visit of King Charles I, the *King's Head* would have been *'one of the finest County' inns in the East Midlands'*. In his book *Timber framed buildings of Nottinghamshire*, Jason Mordan saw that the inn *'was akin to the grandest hotels of our modern cities and played host to royalty'*. Certainly there is evidence to suggest that in mediaeval times English kings did visit and later, in 1646, the visit of King Charles I is very well documented.

Features and layout. Dendrochronological analysis of timbers in the north wing suggest a building date soon after 1476. Apart from the striking outward appearance of the *Saracen's Head*, both upstairs and downstairs have spaces that are highly decorated with impressive late Tudor wall paintings. Two probate inventories dating from 1622 and 1683 show us how wealthy some of the proprietors were and how fashionable some of the inn's furnishings needed to be to attract the patronage of the upper classes.[57] Linen and pewter were essential items for an inn's reputation and inventories show that not only did the *Saracen's Head* possess these items, but silverware, highly valuable bedroom

*A group of **Saracen's** 'regulars', who worked for the Southwell Rural District Council in the late 1930s. Wearing a flat hat and watch chain at the back was 'Gibbo' Whysall from Halam. He would walk every morning from Dunham House for a 'liquid lunch' with his friends Ted Ward and Fred North, who became the local registrar. 'Gibbo' Whysall was related to the England and Nottinghamshire test cricketer, William Whysall. (Ruth Robinson)*

```
A true inventory of all and singular the goods chattels and creditts of Elizabeth
Rippon widow deceased taken and appraised at Southwell the 9th day of
August 1683 by Thomas Rippon Gent and William Lock as followeth
Imprimis   her purse and apparel                          04.0.0
Item                In the Hall
           A fire iron two tables and two formes one cupbord}
           A Lanseckle three chaires and other things      }  02.10.0

                 In the Pewter Buttery
Item       Nineteen Pewter dishes and 3 dozen of Pewter plates}
           7 Pewter Chamber potts 2 basons eleven            }06.00.06
           chandlesticks six salts one cupbord and other things }

Item                In the Great Parlour
           One bedsted with a fetherbed bolster Curtains and  }
           other things belonging to it three tables and carpets }
           one stand one livery cupbord 15 chaires foure stooles } 10.09.00
           and one forme and Fire Iron and tonges and         }
           other things

Item                In the Kitchin
           Eleven Brasse Pannes three skelletts three brasse  }
           potts three brasse mortars & three pestles, Fire Iron }
           Frogs shovell tongs hooks a gallow tree paire of Cobb}09.13.00
           Irons & nine spitts three iron dripping pannes 5 tinn }
           Plates 2 brasse ladles, one wooden platter 3 chaires }
           And 3 stoules and other od things

32.12.06

           Item              In the Larder
           Tenn pewter dishes 4 porringers a dozen Pewter    }
           Spoones One frying Pan Clever one safe and a       }
           chest One Powdring Table one Salt Tubb            } 01.13.06
           One frying Pan Kynnell and Tray Two wooden       }
           platters and other od things                      }

                  In the Brewing House
           One Lead Brewing Tubb one paire of Quernes one    }
           Strike a Brandrith and a fire grate and other lumber } 02.19.00

                  In the Fatte House
           One divers Guile Fatt five th washing truncks one   }
           Kynnell three serges and other lumber             } 01.02.06
```

1683 Inventory on the possessions of victualler, Elizabeth Rippon, *showing ownership of substantial amounts of pewter, carpets and curtains indicating that some innkeepers were amongst the wealthiest citizens of the town. (NA PR/SW 97/17)*

furniture and fashionable curtains as well. The total valuations of the two inventories were £112 and £117 respectively, considerable amounts for the times.

Not surprisingly a 1768 local newspaper refers to the *Saracen's Head* being *'the most commodious Inn'*,[58] and also indicated that it had an extensive innyard. A *1772 indenture* between William Clay of Westhorpe and Richard Ufton, victualler, gave more detail of the inn's immediate surroundings when it referred to Richard Ufton having *'use of the brewhouse, well, croft, orchard, stables and all outbuildings'*.[59] An earlier indenture of 1745 assessed that this whole area of land amounted to five acres. A further indication as to the substantial size of the inn and its even greater prestige by 1821 is revealed in a notice in the *Nottingham Journal* on March 31 of that year, at the height of the coaching era. This reports that the *Saracen's Head* was recognised as a *'Post House'* and had a *'Coach House and Stabling for 50 Horses'*. Clearly, by then it was a leading county inn, taking full advantage of its proximity to the Mansfield-Leadenham turnpike. Meanwhile in 1805, the building of the new Assembly Rooms next door by the architect Richard Ingleman, further added to the inn's appeal, encouraging the leisured classes into town to attend dances, concerts and card games. Eventually, in the 1960s, the Assembly Rooms were integrated into the hotel, being converted into eleven bedrooms. Finally in 1978, the exterior stucco, which had covered the building for nearly 300 years, was removed to reveal the superb half timbered frontage we see today.

Commercial activities. The birth of the coaching age in the late 1700s would have greatly increased commercial activity at the *Saracen's Head*. With its residential accommodation, large yard and good stabling facilities the inn was a natural location for the coaching companies to use for a change of horses. It was situated next to two good routes, the Leadenham-Mansfield turnpike and the Southwell- Nottingham road, and there is clear evidence that in the 1820s up to fifteen coaches a day would drive through the carriageway arch into the *Saracen's Head* yard. The table below, showing only some of the coaches, gives an indication of the bustling activity at the inn and its yard between 1800 and 1845.

Name of Coaches	Coaching Routes	Name of Coaches	Coaching Routes
Accommodation	Newark- Birmingham	Magna Carta	Hull-Nottingham
Champion	Lincoln-Manchester	Tally Ho	Newark-Manchester
No Wonder	Nottingham-Southwell	Queen	Gainsborough-Nottingham
Diligence	Lincoln-Southwell	Pilot	Newark-Nottingham
Omnibus	Southwell-Mansfield	Lady Nelson	Lincoln-Nottingham

Evidence from local newspapers indicates that successive innkeepers seized on the business opportunities which the new coaching age introduced.

> **Nottingham Journal – March 11 1769**
> *This is to acquaint the public that Richard Ufton at the Saracen's Head Inn, has purchased*
> *a very neat New POST CHAISE and good horses, with a sober driver which drives*
> *from Southwell to Nottingham, Mansfield, Newark and elsewhere. Whoever pleases to favour him with*
> *their custom may depend on meeting with civil usage and good entertainment.*
> *By their very humble servant, Richard Ufton (innkeeper).*

Other forms of commerce at the inn.
Before the general establishment of estate agencies and auction houses in the town, the *Saracen's Head* and other inns would have let their 'long room' to auctioneers who dealt in real estate and general trading. In April 1760 a local newspaper recorded that *'a shop belonging to an Apothecary'* was to be sold at the *Saracen's Head*.[60] Private houses were also regularly sold at the *Saracen's Head*, as recorded by the *Nottingham Journal* on the 8th November 1809, when Mrs Byron's house on the Burgage was sold there. In the period from 1809 to 1820 the *Saracen's Head* also featured auctions for two Post Windmills, a Cotton Mill, a Cornmill, and a Ladies' Boarding School. Substantial areas of land were also sold at the inn, such as the auction in July

A play performed at the Assembly Rooms in 1929 by the Wesleyan Girls. The Assembly Rooms were attached to the Saracen's Head Hotel. (Southwell Civic Society)

1809 of the Hockerwood Park Estate [61]. Even livestock on estates was sold, as in June 1815 when the cattle on Burgage Green were auctioned off [62].

From the 1750s regular consignments of London goods came to be sold at Midland inns such as the *Saracen's Head.* These included luxury goods like Derby china, silks, glassware, jewellery, furniture and valuable books and medals. In May 1804 a local auctioneer *'solicits the attention of the Gentry in Southwell to a valuable Collection of books, ancient coins and medals which are to be sold at the Saracen's Head'.*[63] Other types of sales which took place in those years were auctions of knitting frames, furniture and franchises on turnpike tolls.

Social activities. As proprietors of a fashionable 'county' inn, the innkeepers were quick to promote dances, dinners, lectures and concerts for the leisured classes. In the 1700s the *Saracen's Head* regularly held 'Subscription Assemblies', usually dancing and card games, in their Assembly Room. After 1805 Society Balls and Dances came to be held in the new Assembly Rooms, now integrated into the inn. Formal dinners were regularly held at the *Saracen's Head* for the highest echelons of society and official bodies including the Justices of the Peace, local Regimental Officers and Lords Lieutenants. Formal dinners also took place to celebrate special events as recorded in this local newspaper extract

NJ November 4 1809 **Jubilee Celebrations at Southwell**
The Anniversary of the Coronation of GEORGE III was celebrated with those demonstrations of loyalty for which that town is on all occasions eminently conspicuous. At the usual hour Divine Service was attended by the respectable inhabitants of that place. A Ball and Supper followed and was held in the new Assembly Rooms at the Saracen's Head, attended by 80 people, many of whom kept up the dance till nearly 5am.

An administrative centre. In the absence of specialised public buildings in the town such as law courts, post offices and council offices local inns figured very prominently as administrative centres. They acted as bases for local canvassing, whenever elections were contested. Nottinghamshire had the right to send two members to the House of Commons, so the county was divided into north and south divisions, with Southwell in the southern division. In March 1820 a committee room was established at the inn for the canvass and election of Admiral Sotherton. His attributes were outlined in this notice in the Nottingham Journal.

NJ – November 4 1809 **Nottinghamshire Election**
The Central Committee, established at Southwell for the management of Admiral Sotherton's canvass and election, earnestly solicit the cooperation and exertion of the Freeholders of the County of Nottinghamshire on his behalf. Distinguished as the gallant Admiral stands, by every feeling and faculty that can render a man amiable, it is confidently hoped that his undeviating punctuality, his irreproachable integrity and his unblemished deportment will secure the countenance and support of every freeholder.

*An emergency meeting held at the **Saracen's Head** in 1800 in order to decide policies to put down rioting. This was a time of great unrest amongst the labouring classes. (NJ September 6 1800)*

In the later eighteenth century the *Saracen's Head* was one of the principal inns used by the county's authorities as a venue for administering the recruitment of soldiers and sailors to fight overseas against France. From the County Quarter Sessions records we learn that *'For the speedy and effectual recruiting of his Majesty's regiments of foot ... a meeting will take place at the Saracen's Head , Southwell on the 2nd May 1745'.*[64]

Inns had obligations in recruiting and quartering soldiers. Parish officers, usually Parish constables, were to search for persons to be enlisted and if they were unable to provide the numbers required were at risk to be levied themselves! In 1796, during the French Revolutionary War, fifty five men were required for recruitment for the Southwell area.[65] Fines were to be imposed if the recruits were not forthcoming. Furthermore, the *Saracen's Head* was also used as the headquarters for the recuiting and billeting of a local force of militia to be used in emergency situations, for example at times of internal rebellion and invasion. During these turbulent times there was not only the fear of a French invasion but also local unrest amongst the labouring classes, especially in the textile trades, as a result of the threat to craftsmanship ('cut-up' hosiery), which threatened workers' jobs. This notice from a local newspaper in September 1800 of an 'emergency' meeting at the *Saracen's Head,* highlights the point.

Billeting and quartering at inns created much opposition from landlords. Officers would be billeted at county inns and private soldiers at the public houses. Inns could be used for billeting for up to 28 days for the annual training of the local militia. The *Saracen's Head* alone would have up to six officers (and their horses) to accommodate – the allowance given to the innkeeper for food and accommodation was meagre and beer had to be provided free. Not suprisingly, there is much evidence from the innkeepers' written protests that many officers abused the hospitality and overstayed their welcome. How could the innkeepers fight back? There is some suggestion of how they did this in this report of the Returning Officer. *'Many of the small victuallers in the towns and surrounding villages have neither entertainment nor accommodation for either man or horse'.*[66] Could this have been tactical? From 1800 onwards, to the relief of innkeepers everywhere, barracks were built in certain areas of the county.

The *Saracen's Head* would have served a variety of purposes as an administrative centre for the town in the eighteenth and nineteenth centuries. It was the usual venue for the collection of rents due to the Manor of Southwell.

NJ – October 10 1801 **Manor of Southwell**
The great COURT- BARON of his grace the Lord Archbishop of York will be held at the house of William Jones, the Saracen's Head on Saturday October 17th when all the Copyhold Tenants of the Manor, who have not already paid the Quit Rents, are hereby desired to pay the same as well as the arrears to Pentecost, 1801. Dinner on Table at 2 o'clock

Memories of the pre-war, wartime and post-war years. A very human story was passed to me by the granddaughter of a highly successful racecourse trainer, who lived in Kirklington in the period 1920-75. This gentleman enjoyed his regular visits to the *Saracen's Head,* and in the 1940s, with petrol extremely scarce, would come on horseback. On arrival from Kirklington he would give his horse to Fred Dooley, the 'Bootman', who was both barman and yardman. After several drinks at the inn he would collect his horse and make for his Kirklington home. However, according to his granddaughter, there were a number of occasions when only the horse would return, so his family became used to making midnight tours of the ditches and hedge bottoms between Southwell and Kirklington. When petrol became more available, grandfather would visit the *Saracen's Head* by car, although again he couldn't be relied on to return intact. Eventually his family persuaded him to take the Mansfield-Newark bus and because, no doubt, of grandfather's reputation as a successful trainer he was able to make a special 'deal' with the bus driver and conductor. When the last bus to Kirklington stopped at the *Saracen's Head*, the bus conductor would enter the bar to collect grandfather and immediately be served by him with a pint of ale. The old gentleman would then be escorted into the bus and driven to his Kirklington home from where he would re-emerge briefly with either a rabbit or half a dozen eggs, as a token of gratitude for the driver.

A group of the Central Division's Womens' Conservative Association in front of the **Saracen's Head** *in the 1930s, not long after women were finally given the vote. (Anne Reeve)*

According to many senior Southwell residents, the hotel enjoyed a high reputation for its accommodation, not just within the Midland region but also nationally and internationally. Geoff Dodsworth and Dennis Broomfield recall several well known stars in the entertainment business staying there, often when they were appearing in the Nottingham theatres. Geoff Dodsworth remembers that Gert and Daisy Waters would go into the Tap Room at the rear, play darts with the regulars and then drink them under the table! Herbert Lewin's father met Gert and Daisy there and invited them home to Pear Tree Cottage. Herbert recalls his father giving them a rhubarb flower for their buttonholes and that when the sisters left they sang 'Bless this House!' Dennis Broomfield recalls Jack Palance, the American film actor with a 'tough guy' image, also staying at the hotel. In the world of sport it was quite usual for England cricketers, whilst playing at Trent Bridge, to have accommodation at the hotel.

For Nancy Harrison, attending a dance in the Assembly Room was the highlight of the week. She recalls the feelings of anticipation as you walked through the classical entrance and up the elegant staircase onto the dance floor with the musicians' balcony above. Nancy vividly remembers that at the more formal dances the lady was expected to pick up a card from the mantelpiece, which would then be filled in as prospective partners presented themselves for selected dances.

Back in the 1950s and 60s local residents could not always rely on being served. If it happened to be a race night the hotel would be booked up and you would have difficulty getting into the bars. On non-race days the Steward, Ernie, would walk round checking that the gentlemen's dress code was being observed - jacket and tie - and if he didn't like the look of you he was known to say, '*No thank you! Cross the road and take the second door on your right*' (the *Crown*).

Innkeepers. From a 1772 Indenture we learn that William Clay of Westhorpe entered into an agreement to let the *Saracen's Head* to innkeepers, Richard Ufton and G. Flower. Amongst the issues agreed were the following '*Each of them (Ufton and Flower) will keep a good Post Chaise...There will be sale of Ale, beer, Cyder, Porter or Perry,...They will have use of the brewhouse, well, croft, orchard, stables and all outbuildings'.*[67] Two of Richard Ufton's successors, William Hind and William Thompson, were not slow to 'market' themselves and their inn, as the following notices show.

NJ March 27 1779 William Thompson late of the Crown Inn, Southwell, takes this method to inform his friends he has removed hence to the Saracen's Head ... which he has improved and fitted up in a genteel manner. The hotel is now rendered very agreeable, being well supplied with new beds; the stables greatly improved...He has laid in a good stock of Old Red Port and other New Wines. He returns his most sincere thanks to his old friends for their past favours and hopes for their future encouragement.

It is interesting to note that William Thompson has '*graduated*' from the *Crown* to the *Saracen's Head*. There is plenty of evidence of this practice of publicans rising up through the hierarchy of inns in the town. William Thompson was followed by William Hind, who showed he was a man of substance and patriotism in 1794 when he gave a generous donation to 'Loyal Aids' for the purpose of raising a local corps of cavalry. He, too, shows a shrewd, entrepreneurial mind when he seizes on the temporary closure of a nearby inn, the *Cross Keys*, to solicit the favours of their regular clients.

Between the wars the innkeeper, Fred Heald, an ex-butler from Welbeck Abbey, was very much a perfectionist. Fred couldn't abide creases in anything and he even instructed his wife to iron his newspaper before breakfast. If Fred was not satisfied he would send the paper back. Some years later, Fred's son fell from a *Saracen's* bedroom window when drunk, killing himself.

NJ -February 16 1788 William Hind of the Saracen's Head , Southwell, begs leave to inform his numerous friends and the public that his highest wish is still to merit their favours and approbation. And whereas the Cross Keys Inn is now shut up, he shall esteem happy in accommodating such Gentlemen who formerly frequented that house …. no exertions will be spared to render the Saracen's Head perfectly commodious and agreeable in every department. NB. Southwell is in the direct road from Norfolk, Cambridgeshire and to Matlock, Buxton, Manchester and Liverpool. There are Neat Post Chaises with able horses

Reputedly the room where King Charles I spent his last hours of freedom before his arrest. (Stuart Blackwood)

A royal visit. Not suprisingly, much interest has always surrounded the historic visit of King Charles I on that fateful day of May 5th 1646. Evidence shows that by May 1646 the position of the king and his Royalist army was desperate. They had suffered a series of setbacks, culminating in the decisive defeat at Naseby in June 1646. Whilst in Oxford, which was encircled by Parliamentarian troops, he decided to escape and make an agreement with the Scottish Army that was laying siege to the Royalist town of Newark. Charles was employing a French diplomat, Montreuil, resident at the *King's Arms* (*Saracen's Head*), to negogiate with the Scots, who Charles expected would be more accommodating than the Parliamentarian army. When Montreuil sent an encouraging message to Charles, he set off with two loyal attendants from Oxford in disguise, beard cut off and dressed as a clergyman.

The dramatic account of what happened next once King Charles I arrived at the inn is given by the historian RP Shilton in his *History of Southwell* (1818).

On the south side of the gateway, was an apartment, consisting of dining-room and bedroom. This apartment, Montreville (Montreuil) occupied til the king came, when he gave it up to him. The inhabitants still talk of it as the King's Bedchamber. The King sent for the Scottish Commissioners, who occupied the Palace, before dinner, and dined with them at this Inn. Here he gave himself up to them, and in the afternoon, went under escort of their army to Kelham.

Thus King Charles I spent his last hours of freedom at the *Saracen's Head* before becoming a prisoner of David Leslie, the Scottish army commander, who then escorted the king northwards and, despite earlier promises, handed him over to the English Parliament in exchange for the waiver of a loan. The two rooms on the ground floor to the left of the arch which the king used have now been made into one, with a dining area as before and a lounge replacing the former bedroom.

Strange happenings. But the story of this well known event in our history does not end here. Whenever you visit the *Saracen's Head* today you are reminded of this drama by the many fine prints and drawings around the rooms, which refer to the presence of King Charles I at the old inn. But more than that, over a period of many years, some residents have commented on strange happenings in the middle of the night, which have been linked by some people to the sad fate of King Charles. Within the King Charles Suite there have been reports of strange noises in the early hours, particularly of young children running up the corridor. Other observations have focused on the sudden appearance of orbs, small white lights, on the prints around the room. Down the corridor in Room 4 guests have referred to unusual changes of temperature in the room, of doors locking and unlocking and of the television being turned off and on without explanation. In most of these reported cases it has been felt the 'spiritual presence' was benign, however, on some occasions it has led guests to check out in the middle of the night.

Two other 'presences' have been reported at the old inn over the years. According to the *Saracen's Head's* own leaflet '*the Grey Lady lurks in the Ladies toilets, powdering her beautiful face whilst captivatingly laughing and tunefully whistling happily'*. I was informed by one of the management team that some members of staff will not use the toilet after an unexplained incident when a member of staff was punched in the stomach, landing on the floor, at a time when there was no-one else in the room. The second 'presence' seems to be far more benign. There have been a number of unexplained happenings downstairs over the years reported by successive Night Porters, such as someone knocking at doors late at night and someone turning on the microwave oven and other electrical appliances when there is no-one around. Tradition at the Saracen's Head is that this is the work of '*Old Tom, a Regency gent, who with powdered wig and flared cuffs, shuffles both upstairs and down, searching for a card game'*.

Brewing ale. The *Saracen's Head* brewed its own ale for very many years but by the late nineteenth century most inns and public houses found this practice was no longer commercially viable. Many of these inns became tied to local breweries. Until 1932 the *Saracen's Head* was owned by a series of Nottingham businesses and then later in that year was taken over by James Hole and Co., the Newark Brewery, who remained in control until the 1970s.

Wheatsheaf

Situation. The *Wheatsheaf* stands in King Street next to the modern Market Square. There has been a public house here since the early 1700s and whilst it remains a reasonably sized building today, in times past it had considerably more land at the rear, primarily for the use of the village carriers when they brought their waggons and horses into the innyard.

*The **Wheatsheaf** in the early 1900s. Note the Warwick and Richardson Brewery sign and the cottages to the left where the Market Square is now. (Southwell Civic Society.)*

Structural alterations. Despite the changes the *Wheatsheaf* has retained much of its original character, particularly in the public bar, the room closest to King Street, where the low ceilings and timber framed structure give a feeling of age and comfort. Geoff Dodsworth, a regular for over forty years, recalls that the tap room or public bar was at the back and the front room was the lounge. Most of the present lounge bar has been added at a later time and would have been originally used as living accommodation for the landlord and his family. Geoff Dodsworth also remembers when a serving hatch was in use just inside the entrance from the Market Square. On the first floor the *Wheatsheaf* had for many years its own Assembly Room, used for parties, concerts and local group meetings. So many public houses in the town had Assembly Rooms but when one considers how few public buildings there were, and how limited the choice of entertainment, then it is not so surprising that the public house assembly room was a popular amenity. When structural alterations were made in the 1970s on the first floor, the workers came across fragments of Edwardian wallpaper commemorating the coronation of King George V in 1910. On the second floor there are two small rooms with fireplaces. It is possible that around 1800, during the wars with France, soldiers were billeted there. Landlords were obliged to take in soldiers for a meagre allowance and the practice was to give the soldiers the most basic accommodation, so discouraging a long stay. At the back of the building, according to newspaper accounts of auctions in 1810 and 1820, there were extensive cellars, a brewhouse, various outbuildings and a big garden where pigs were kept for many years.

> *NJ January 3 1820* **Wheatsheaf Public House** *To Be Sold at Auction, at the Saracen's Head.*
> *That well built good accustomed public house in Southwell known by the*
> *Sign of the Wheatsheaf late in the occupation of Mr.Charles Brailsford and now of his under tenant.*
> *There is an extensive Garden and other Conveniences which make it desirable Property for a Maltster,*
> *Butcher or any other Profession connected with an Innkeeper, where room is essential*

*Three **Wheatsheaf** regulars in the 1980s – Bob Greaves, Matt Grundy and Ted Hamilton. (Larry and Di Dukes.)*

Social activities. In 1794 we have evidence from *Nottinghamshire County Records of the Eighteenth Century* that Friendly Societies met regularly at the *Wheatsheaf*.[68] Friendly Societies, which aimed to help their members provide for future medical bills or funeral expenses, found the public houses a cheap, convenient and congenial rendezvous. The availablity of facilities such as a bar and private room where cards and dominoes could be played, would make public houses like the *Wheatsheaf* a natural home for charitable and friendly societies. The usual procedure on these 'club' nights would be that every member would pay a few pence, half of which would be spent on beer whilst the remainder was passed to the steward, (who might well have been the landlord) to be deposited in a box to raise a fund for the relief of members who required money in cases of sickness or emergency.

Wartime and post-war memories. Jock Grant recalls 'Pop' Berry being the landlord and at the same time working for the Electricity Board during the Second World War. He recalls that there were gaslights in both rooms and that 'Pop' served beer by jugs straight from the barrel. Geoff Dodsworth remembers when there was a hatch by the entrance with two stools for people who either wanted to take beer away in a jug or who preferred to sit and drink the beer there rather than go into a room. Playing in the Skittle Alley was one of the popular pastimes of regulars at this time.

In the 1970s Bob Greaves used to entertain with his spoon playing. Invariably he would be accompanied by 'Nipper' who for many years ran the market and lived nearby in a caravan. Malcolm Greaves, Bob's nephew, is another *Wheatsheaf* regular and he had a taste of the big time when 'his scriptwriter', Southwell's William Ivory, chose to make Malcolm the central character of his television series, *Common as Muck*. When Billy wrote his script, he drew on his experiences of working with Malcolm as a refuse collector, and incorporated aspects of this in two characters, played by the well known actors, Edward Woodward and Tim Healey. When I spoke to Malcolm about this claim to fame he said that Billy Ivory had been very keen to have the series filmed around Southwell. However, the producer wanted Manchester so eventually a compromise was made with the filming taking place in Manchester but with local Southwell names like Easthorpe and Shady Lane being used in the script.

Landlords. Thomas Mansford (c.1792-1810) was very much at the heart of town activities at that time and this included his close involvement with local Friendly Societies. One of Thomas Mansford's successors, William Geeson, who was also a flaxdresser, joined the *Loyal Southwell Volunteer Infantry* in 1804 at a time when a French invasion was feared.[69] It is of interest how patriotic and public spirited many publicans were in this turbulent period, when invasion and revolution at home were seen as likely occurrences. An interesting story centres on a later landlord, Richard Revill, who was an exceptionally fat man. He unfortunately died at a relatively young age and after the mourners had failed to manoeuvre the big coffin out of the main door, they resorted to taking out the front window to get access to King Street. Later, in the mid Victorian period, the families of two landlords, Thomas Dunstan and William Adamson, ran bakery businesses in the town. Clearly, these multiple occupations helped to provide a more comfortable income for the landlord.

Closer to our own times two families stand out for long service. Abraham and Maria Goosemann ran the *Wheatsheaf* from 1906 to 1926 and they were followed by Harold Bunting Berry and his wife, who were there from 1926 to 1955. According to Geoff Dodsworth one of the landlords in the 1960s was obsessed with chamber pots. He had them hanging from the beams in the bar and at closing time he would clang one of them with a spoon and shout, *'Come on, piss off'.*

Brewing ale. Sale notices in the early nineteenth century inform us that the *Wheatsheaf* had its own brewhouse but by the end of the century the licensing records tell us that the WS Davy's Devon Brewery from Newark had taken over the public house. In 1926 another Newark brewery, the well known Warwick and Richardson's, bought out WS Davy and remained in possession until the 1970s. Old photographs show the Newark brewery advertisements on the side of the public house.

10. Conclusion

It is clear that the inns and alehouses played a major role in the social, commercial and administrative life of Southwell during this period. The number and variety of their services was astonishing, touching upon most aspects of town life and providing benefits for the publicans and often for the community at large.

In the eighteenth and nineteenth centuries the inns and alehouses were the social hub of the town. For the 'leisured classes' inns provided and promoted concerts, balls, public dinners, travelling theatre and sporting activities. For the labouring poor, *'they offered...their sole recreational institution and, moreover, served a number of useful functions, as pawn shops or labour exchanges for example. Thus the alehouse was not only a place to go and drink, but also a location where neighbourly and communal solidarities might be re-affirmed.*[70]

In this same period, inns and alehouses were important centres for commercial activity. Before the establishment of estate agencies, auction rooms and retail shops, inns and alehouses featured sales and auctions of anything from real estate to books and antique coins, silverware, furniture and carpets. Equally important to the town was the role the inns and alehouses played in the carrying and coaching trades. The diversity of their services was remarkable, ranging from offering facilities to long and short-distance carriers to the supply of private post-chaises and the full development of coaching. Several innkeepers enlarged and adapted their premises to accommodate coaches and gentlemen's horses.

The administrative role of the inns and alehouses was also very important in the development of the town in the eighteenth and nineteenth centuries. In the absence of public buildings such as law courts, post offices, police stations and financial centres, local inns and some alehouses acted as centres for the conducting of public business. Not only did publicans provide their services for an astonishingly wide range of legal, financial and business enterprises, but many publicans took an active part in these enterprises. Some innkeepers were turnpike trustees, whilst others were tax collectors, post-masters and members of the Association for the Prosecution of Felons.

Advertisement from WS Davy Brewery, Newark. This brewery took over the **Wheatsheaf** *in the early 1900s.*

However, by the mid to late nineteenth century, the growth of retail shops and public buildings, coupled with the increase of independent businesses, led to a decline in the use of local inns for commercial and administrative purposes. Importantly too, there were definite signs of an economic decline in the town, partly attributable to a fall in the population linked with the growth of employment opportunities outside the town. At the same time, a religious revival led to a hardening of attitudes to the drink trade and drunkenness, resulting in local magistrates' being more strict in the granting of licences and in the closure of a number of public houses.

Nevertheless, the inns and alehouses remained the social hub of the town and still exercised, as they do to this day, a substantial influence on the general culture and ethos of the local community. Equally, the publicans continued to form a valuable section of the community, many carrying on the traditions of being both enterprising landlords and also leaders of social and economic developments within their neighbourhoods. It is reassuring to know, when you consider the large range of social and commercial activities that take place in our public houses today, that these traditions still remain with us.

11. Glossary

Historically, there were three main types of establishment for the sale of alcoholic drink: the **inn**, the **tavern** and the **alehouse.** All three had their origins in the medieval period and were the designations used in a government survey of 1577, which provides the first detailed information we have on drinking places. Many documents interpret these terms strictly whereas others are very loose in their definition.

Inn

An inn is a building whose primary purpose is to provide accommodation and food for travellers. In the Middle Ages this form of hospitality was traditionally performed by monasteries or the houses of the nobility. By the sixteenth century inns had taken over these functions, being licensed by magistrates to sell beer and wine. In later years many of the larger inns became more commonly known as hotels.

Tavern

Taverns were usually found in large towns and cities and therefore do not feature in this book which is centred on a small town in a predominantly rural area. Taverns, licensed by the local magistrates to sell beer and wine, were often the haunts of the professional classes.

Alehouse

In 1700 there were far more alehouses than inns and taverns. They had developed over the years as the basic, everyday, social drinking place for working men. An alehouse was often simply a room - for example a kitchen or parlour in a domestic dwelling, frequently run by women for the labouring classes. Alehouses had a poor reputation and were often dirty, crowded places, often associated with crime. Magistrates' records frequently refer to the worst of the alehouses as 'tippling' houses. Although many alehouses were licensed by the magistrates many were not, and simply hoped the authorities would turn a blind eye. This makes it difficult to determine the exact numbers of alehouses.

Beerhouse

Beerhouses were introduced as a result of the 1830 Beer Act. The government was keen to encourage the working classes to drink beer rather than spirits, especially gin. The act permitted any householder to pay a two guinea excise fee and open a beerhouse without having to apply for a magistrate's licence. As with earlier alehouses, most beerhouses consisted of one room in a small dwelling or craftsman's workshop. By the 1860s when successive governments came under pressure to restrict the number of licensed premises, many beerhouses closed or raised their status to public houses.

Public house

The precise origin of the term 'public house' is unclear but it is likely that it derived simply from a contraction of 'public alehouse'. The term only came into common usage after 1854. A public house is seen as a building licensed to sell beer and spirits, where specialist rooms are provided for different purposes and classes (ie. saloon bar and taproom).

Hotel

The term 'hotel' derives from the French word describing a large mansion or public building. By the 1850s, with the increase in affluence amongst the propertied classes, many travellers expected to stay in more comfortable establishments devoted to the provision of accommodation. This led to some of the larger inns either 'upgrading' themselves as hotels, (like the *Admiral Rodney* and the *Crown*), or retaining the term 'inn' and merely adding the word 'hotel' as the *Saracen's Head* did. The *Newcastle Arms*, by contrast, was built after the heyday of the coaching age and so was never associated with being an inn. From its earliest days it adopted the term 'hotel' as it offered accommodation for travellers, primarily those using the railway.

Ale

Ale was made solely from cereals (barley), artificially germinated, then moved to a heated kiln.

Beer

Beer was made by adding hops to the above process. This practice came from the Netherlands in the fifteenth century.

12. Abbreviations

NAd	Newark Advertiser newspaper
NA	Nottinghamshire Archives
NH	Nottingham Herald newspaper
NJ	Nottingham Journal newspaper
NNM	Nottingham and Newark Mercury newspaper
NUMD	University of Nottingham, Department of Manuscripts and Special Collections.
NR	Nottingham Review
NWE	Nottingham Weekly Express

13. Select Bibliography

Arundel B	*Southwell-A History Walk,* Newark and Sherwood, 1988.
Austin M	*Under the Heavy Clouds,* Cardiff, 2004.
Becher Rev'd JT	*Rules and Regulations of Southwell Friendly Institution (1823),* preface.
Bennett N	*The Journey of King Charles I into Captivity,* Lincoln Cathedral Publications, 1999.
Bone R	*The Inns of Nottingham, Derby and Leicester,* MA Thesis, Leicester, 1985
Cousins R	*Newark Inns and Public Houses,* Nottinghamshire County Council, 1991.
Hardstaff R	*Georgian Diary- Southwell (1781),* Southwell and District LHS, 2000.
Hardstaff R and Lyth P	*Georgian Southwell,* Newark and Sherwood DC, 1986.
Haydon P	*An Inebriated History of Britain,* Sutton Publishing, 2005.
Heathcote BV	*Viewing the Lifeless Body,* Nottinghamshire County Council, 2005.
Hemingway G	*The Coaching and Posting Inns of Newark,* 1977.
Henson G	*History of the Framework Knitters* (1831), Nottingham.
Hustwayte M, Young P	*Holy Trinity Church, Southwell* (1846-96)
Jennings P	*The Local – A History of the English Pub,* Tempus Publishing, 2007.
Jones M	*The Secret Middle Ages,* 2003.
Lawrence DH	*Women in Love (1920), Cambridge University Press,* 1987
Local Writers	*Southwell-The Town and Its People,* Southwell and District LHS, 1992.
Local Writers	*Southwell- The Town and Its People Vol. 2,* Southwell and District LHS, 2006
Marcombe D	*English Small Town Life - Retford (1520-1642),* 1993.
Marshall DS	*The History of Brewing in Newark-on-Trent,* Acorn Publications, 2000.
Mordan J	*The Timber-Frame Buildings of Nottinghamshire,* Nottinghamshire County Council, 2004.
Notts.County Council	*Nottinghamshire County Records of the Eighteenth Century*
Pask B	*Newark the Bounty of Beer,* Nottinghamshire County Council, 1997.
Putman R	*Beers and Breweries of Britain,* Shire Publications, 2004.
Rowley JJ	*Drink and the Public House in Nottingham,* Thoroton Society, 1975.
Sharpe JA	*Early Modern England: A Social History,* 1997.
Shilton RP	*History of Southwell* (1818), Nottinghamshire County Council, 1993
Shire Wood Ranger	*Our Nottinghamshire Villages* (1894).
Summers N	*A Prospect of Southwell,* Kelham House Publications 1974.
Walker A	*Aspects of Lincoln,* Wharncliffe Books, 2001.
West M	*A Westhorpe Anthology,* Mary West, 1989.

14. References

1. RP Shilton, *History of Southwell* (1818), 56-7.

2. *NJ* 6 April 1782.

3. NA PR/SW 50/11 *Inventory of Francis Clarke, 1622*.

4. NA PR/SW 97/17 *Inventory of Elizabeth Rippon, 1683*.

5. White's *Nottinghamshire Directory* (1832).

6. *Derby Mercury* 7 June 1765.

7. G Winter, *A Country Camera* (1844-1914), 1.

8. *NJ* 25 February 1769.

9. *NJ* 6 January, 1821.

10. RP Shilton, *History of Southwell* (1818), 293.

11. Guildhall Library, London, *Sun Fire Office Registers*, Volume 293, Policy number 444523

12. *Nottinghamshire County Records of the Eighteenth Century, Armed Forces,* 262.

13. *NJ* 29 Sept. 1821, *NJ* 16 July 1814, *NJ* 17 December 1803, *NJ* 28 September 1816.

14. NA DD/M 71/200/2 etc

15. J Lawson, *Progress in Pudsey (*1818), 83-4.

16. *Life of John Holmes 1821-99*, manuscript in private ownership.

17. J Lawson, *Progress in Pudsey (*1818), 84-5.

18. A Patrick, *Maltings in Nottinghamshire* (1977).

19. Brewery History Society - *Century of British Brewers 1890-2004.*

20. *NJ* 17 February, 1810.

21. *The Reminisences of Richard Fisher 1878-1966,* typescript kindly lent by Mary West.

22. White's *Nottinghamshire Directory* (1832).

23. NA PS/B 10/1 *Sale of the Black Bull Inn* 1908.

24. NA DD/M 90/17 *Abstract of Title, James Maltby.*

25. *NJ* 3 May 1783.

26. NA DD/M 71/322 *Valuation- The Castle Inn* (1802).

27. White's *Nottinghamshire Directory* (1832).

28. NA DD/M 71/121 *Deeds, ancient public house, Farthing Street.*

29. *NJ* 25 February, 1815.

30. *NWE* 17 June 1887.

31. Brewery History Society, *Century of British Brewers* 1890-2004.

32. Friedrich's Gazeteer,*The Breweries of the British Isles.*

33. NA DD/M 71/247 *Plan of White Swan Inn* 1921.

34. Borthwick Institute CP. H.4549, 1697 *Chancery Court Records.*

35. White's *Nottinghamshire Directory,* 1832 and 1844.

36. DD/844/1-4 *William IV, Maythorne Cottages* (1961-77).

37. DD/844/1-4 *William IV, Maythorne Cottages* (1961-77).

38. Census 1881,1891.

39. R.Hardstaff, *Georgian Diary,* (2000), 65.

40. Pigot's *Nottinghamshire Directory* (1841).

41. R.Hardstaff, *Georgian Diary,* (2000), 40.

42. NA DD/M 71/200/2.

43. NA C/Q/DC 3/6 *Petition against the system of Rural Police* 1842.

44. RP Shilton, *History of Southwell* (1818), 294.

45. Pigot's *Nottinghamshire Directory* (1819).

46. *NJ* 1 June 1822.

47. R.Hardstaff, *Georgian Diary,* (2000), 43.

48. R.Hardstaff, *Georgian Diary,* (2000), 43.

49. *NJ* 10 November 1787.

50. *NJ* 14 November 1789.

51. *Life of John Holmes 1821-99*

52. *Universal Directory of Great Britain 1791.*

53. BV Heathcote, *Viewing the Lifeless Body,* 2005.

54. NA DD/M 112/219 *Will of William Smedley, innkeeper,* (1887).

55. NA DD/M 71/225 *Sale Bill, Reindeer Inn, Westgate* (1847).

56. *NJ* 21 November 1812.

57. NA PR/SW 50/11 *Inventory of Francis Clarke* (1622) and NA PR/SW 97/17 *Inventory of Elizabeth Rippon* (1683).

58. *NJ* 3 September 1768.

59. NA DD/M 71/332-335 *Indenture William Clay* (1772).

60. *NJ* 19 April 1760.

61. *NJ* 1 July 1809.

62. *NJ* 10 June 1815.

63. *NJ* 5 May 1804.

64. Notts.CC Records of the Eighteenth Century - *County Quarter Sessions Records,* 262.

65. Notts.CC Records of the Eighteenth Century, Armed Forces, 262.

66. TNA, 1756 Billeting Returns, WO 30/49.

67. NA DD/M 71/332-335.

68. *Nottinghamshire County Records of the Eighteenth Century* (Rules and Regulations of Friendly Societies), 351.

69. RP Shilton, *History of Southwell* (1818), 298.

70. JA Sharpe, *Early Modern England: A Social history* (1997), 291-2.